PENNSYLVANIA'S
SUSQUEHANNA

PENNSYLVANIA'S SUSQUEHANNA

Interesting history, legends and descriptions of the "heart river" of Pennsylvania—its surrounding hills and mountains, its broad valleys and narrow gorges, its canals and railroads, its towns and cities and, above all, its beauty

BY

ELSIE SINGMASTER

HARRISBURG, PENNSYLVANIA

J. HORACE McFARLAND COMPANY

1950

Copyright 1950, by
J. HORACE McFARLAND COMPANY
HARRISBURG, PENNSYLVANIA

Wholly produced by
J. HORACE McFARLAND COMPANY
MOUNT PLEASANT PRESS
HARRISBURG, PA.

To my friend Alice R. Eaton

CONTENTS

Pennsylvania's Susquehanna 1

    Drains half the area of Commonwealth. The Indians of the Susquehanna valley. Indian names remain mostly as names of streams. A wealth of native shrubs and flowers along its course. Trees line the shores and clothe the surrounding hills. Remains of abandoned canals, the ever-present railroads and airplanes overhead. River lore gathered from many sources.

The North Branch 11

    The Great Bend enters Pennsylvania and returns to New York State. Enters the state again to the west and is joined by Chemung River at Tioga Point. White men on river in 1616. The exploration of Etienne Brulé. German emigrants journey from the Hudson in search for better land. Conrad Weiser, one of emigrants, Indian interpreter, friend of Chief Shikellamy and guide to Lewis Evans, maker of maps, Count von Zinzendorf, Moravian missionary and John Bartram, botanist. Sullivan's expedition during the American Revolution. The story of Asylum, a refuge prepared for Marie Antoinette. Wyalusing Rocks, Indian lookout. Meshoppen and Tunkhannock. The anthracite coal region, the mines and miners. The Wyoming Valley and the Wyoming massacre. Wilkes-Barre, chief city of the North Branch. The towns of Nanticoke, Shickshinny, Wapwallopen, Berwick, Bloomsburg, with its State Teachers' College, and Danville. Sunbury at the junction with the West Branch of the Susquehanna.

The West Branch 53

    Source in the central plateau of Pennsylvania; drains a wild, sparsely inhabited region of forests. Probably visited by Etienne Brulé in his exploration. Conrad Weiser used lower reaches in journeys with Chief Shikellamy to Six Nations council at Onondaga. Members of half-Indian Montour family, friendly to white settlers. Upper reaches of West Branch habitat of "quality" white pine. Forest wealth rafted for many years from Cherry Tree to the Chesapeake. Region, now in second-growth forest, abounds in large and small game. Some stretches of river almost inaccessible. The story of Jerry Church, founder of Lock Haven. Williamsport, chief city of the West Branch, once a "lumber city," now prosperous with diversified manufacture. The great rafts of 100 years ago; the log booms of Lock Haven and Williamsport. The McMaster account of the 1889 Flood. Many hillsides now reforested by the State and private interests. The Declaration of Independence from George III under the Tiadaghton Elm. The towns and creeks below Williamsport. Bucknell University at Lewisburg. The meeting with the North Branch at Northumberland.

The Juniata 93

    A generally placid stream, brown rather than "blue" as in old song. Its source in southern Pennsylvania. The forests of the Juniata basin. Bedford Springs—a place for recreation for many famous men. The Raystown Branch spirals north through the mountains. The Frankstown Branch, parallel, but farther west. The Little Juniata swings west at Tyrone. The town of Huntingdon—site of Juniata College—once called Standing Stone from Indian monolith. Jack's Narrows and hillsides at Mt. Union scarred by open quarries furnishing material for refractories. Lewistown at the junction of Kishacoquillas Creek. The Lewistown Narrows and the Pennsylvania Railroad. The river in a widening valley continues past Mifflintown, Port Royal, Thompsontown, Millerstown and Amity Hall to Clark's Ferry where it joins the Susquehanna.

CONTENTS

PAGE

The Main River—Northumberland to Harrisburg 115

Northumberland, home of Joseph Priestley, discoverer of oxygen. Joining of the North and West branches—a region of exceptional beauty. Here passed Etienne Brulé, Conrad Weiser, Lewis Evans and John Bartram on early trips of discovery. The danger of flood and protection by dikes. Sunbury on the site of Indian Shamokin, abode of Chief Shikellamy, sachem of the Iroquois. Thomas Edison, at Sunbury, erected the first three-wire central-station electric plant. South of Sunbury a new electric generating plant using residue coal. Selinsgrove—site of Susquehanna University—partly on Isle of Que, once property of Conrad Weiser. Tales of Herndon, Port Trevorton and McKees Half Falls. Remains of Susquehanna Canal visible along road. Liverpool and its broad view of river and mountains. The cliff called Girty's Face. New Buffalo and Amity Hall where travelers have stopped for more than a century. Two islands, where Juniata joins, were Indian villages. Clark's Ferry site of old ferry, later used as canal crossing with boats towed from bridge above dam. Two picturesque main highways south from Clark's Ferry. The Rockville Bridge, longest stone-arch railroad bridge in the world. Harrisburg—capital of Pennsylvania—at crossing of The Great Valley, site of John Harris' trading post and ferry. The site of the "Camelback" Bridge, one of four famous bridges built by Theodore Burr. The Susquehanna, Harrisburg's river, glorified by miles of river parks. An old description of the river at Harrisburg from "Picturesque America."

Canals, Steamboats and Pirates 163

Still can be traced along banks of main river and its branches. Canals first proposed by William Penn and endorsed by Robert Fulton. Building spurred by success of New York's Erie Canal. Pennsylvania Canal a combination of water and rail including the "Portage Railroad" crossing the Alleghenies. General routes of canals and problems of construction. Charles Dickens' description of canal trip from Harrisburg to Pittsburgh. A pleasure outing on the canal boat *Comfort* of Harrisburg. Towns made prosperous by canal-boat trade. Attempts made to navigate Susquehanna by steamboat ended in failure. Some steamboats used on pool of Shamokin Dam at Sunbury. Canal boats attacked by bands of thieves or "pirates." Steam railroads doomed the canals and forced abandonment.

The Main River—Harrisburg to the Maryland Border 175

The grave of John Harris, the trader. Steelton and the Bethlehem Steel plant. Middletown at mouth of Swatara Creek eastern waterway of the Great Valley. The Cumberland Valley and the Conodoguinet and Yellow Breeches (Shawnee) creeks. Hill Island, one of few elevated islands of river. The York Haven power development. Unusual potholes in river bed at Conewago Falls. Two Conewago creeks and the Codorus Creek. A series of wild glens on the west bank. Marietta, famous in rafting days. Chickies Rock, a landmark. The more-than-a-mile-long concrete bridge from Columbia to Wrightsville on site of Burr bridge. Overview of Long Level (Conejohela) from dairy farm. Section once claimed by both Pennsylvania and Maryland; settled by Mason and Dixon survey. River south of Columbia bordered by picturesque wooded hills backed by fat farms of Lancaster and York counties, to east and west. Susquehanna likened to Rhine for beauty. McCalls Ferry, narrowest part of main river. Bridge built here by Theodore Burr an outstanding feat of engineering in wood. Pools of power dams at Safe Harbor, Holtwood and Conowingo much used for recreation. Lower stretches of river difficult to reach by roads. View of great beauty from Cutler's Point looking toward Maryland. Mount Johnson Island, sanctuary for the bald eagle—emblematic bird of American freedom. The Peach Bottoms, site of farthest south ferry in Pennsylvania. Tribute from the pen of Lloyd Mifflin.

Index 230

At Dauphin Narrows, above Harrisburg, the Susquehanna flows through a second gap in the mountains. US 22 runs close to the river so that travelers can see the sparkling water and tree-clad mountains. To the left is the southern spur of Cove Mountain; in the distance the northern spur of Cove Mountain and Peters Mountain frame the gap at Clark's Ferry.

Photo: R. B. McFarland

"And when I had asked the name of the river from the brakeman, and heard that it was called the Susquehanna, the beauty of the name seemed to be part and parcel of the beauty of the land. As when Adam with divine fitness named the creatures, so this word Susquehanna was at once accepted by the fancy. That was the name, as no other could be, for that shining river and desirable valley."

—Robert Louis Stevenson
"Across the Plains," 1879

LIST OF ILLUSTRATIONS

                             PAGE

In Dauphin Narrows, *Frontispiece* x

PENNSYLVANIA'S SUSQUEHANNA

From West Fairview xiv
Mountain Laurel, the State Flower 2
Native Rhododendron 4
Hepatica, herald of spring 5
White drifts of Dogwood 7
Mertensia or Virginia Bluebell 8

THE NORTH BRANCH

The River enters Pennsylvania 10
Starrucca Viaduct. 12
Near Oakland 15
Sayre and Athens from air 16
Upstream from Athens 18
South of Wysox 19
Tioga Point 20
North of Towanda 23
Standing Stone 24
Overlooking site of Asylum 26
Wyalusing Rocks 28
South of Wyalusing 30
Great Elm at Laceyville 31
From Tunkhannock Bridge 32
In the vicinity of Falls 35
Campbell's Ledge 36
Pittston from West Pittston 37
Wilkes-Barre from air 38
Wilkes-Barre and bridge 40
Coal breaker at Plymouth 41
Tilsbury's Knob, West Nanticoke 42
South from Shickshinny 43
Falls in Ricketts Glen 45
Upriver from Wapwallopen 46
At East Bloomsburg 48
River Park, Danville 49
From Mile Hill, Sunbury 50

THE WEST BRANCH
                             PAGE

At Cherry Tree, a mountain stream 52
A sharp bend at McGees Mills 54
Near Mahaffey 55
Approaching Curwensville 56
Ferns in West Branch forest 57
River park, Clearfield 58
Road and river near Shawville 60
Looking toward Surveyor 61
Afternoon shadows, Karthaus 62
South of Keating 63
View from Hyner Bridge 64
Along picturesque US Route 120 67
White Pines, West Branch wealth 68
Joe-Pye-Weed in midsummer 69
Park and bridge, Lock Haven 70
Hemlock, the State Tree 72
Near Antes Fort 74
From Jersey Shore 74
Tiadaghton Elm 76
Old log boom at Williamsport 77
Williamsport from air 78
Montoursville from US Route 15 80
Eagles Mere, peerless Pennsylvania lake . . 82
The Muncy Hills from Montgomery . . . 85
River front and bridge, Watsontown . . . 86
From Oak Heights, south of Milton 88
River at Lewisburg 90
Elder along stream 91

THE JUNIATA

Near Aliquippa Gap 92
Upstream from Hopewell 94
Approaching Saxton 95
Frankstown Branch at Water Street 96
From Bridge below Huntingdon 98
Jack's Narrows from Sideling Hill 100
West from Newton-Hamilton 102
Near McVeytown 103

xii

LIST OF ILLUSTRATIONS

	PAGE
Along Penna. Route 103 beyond Lewistown	104
Juniata River and Lewistown	106
Lewistown Narrows from west	108
Downstream from Port Royal	110
From bridge, Millerstown	111
At junction with the Susquehanna	112

NORTHUMBERLAND TO HARRISBURG

River junction at Northumberland	114
River in flood at Sunbury	116
Shikellamy Cliff from Sunbury	117
Canoeing at Selinsgrove	119
Isle of Que, where Penns Creek joins	120
North of Herndon	123
Downriver from Dalmatia	124
Shadbush in spring	125
Overlooking Dalmatia from south	126
From Fisher Ridge north of Millersburg	128
Trailing Arbutus	129
River Ferry, Millersburg	130
South from Millersburg	130
Panorama from Liverpool	132–133
Bed of old canal, New Buffalo	134
River and mountains, Juniata Bridge	136
Clark's Ferry and Juniata Bridges	138
South of Duncannon	140
The river from Peters Mountain	143
Dauphin Narrows from fire tower	144
Islands and river near Perdix	146
Hillside of Wild Phlox	147
Rockville Bridge from west	148
Marysville from Dauphin County shore	150
South from Rockville Bridge arch	151
Gaps and bridge, north of Harrisburg	152
The river boulevard, Harrisburg	155
Bathing Beach, Harrisburg	156
Kipona Sports, Harrisburg	158
Memorial Day Boat Races, Wormleysburg	159
Sailing on the river, Harrisburg	161

CANALS, STEAMBOATS AND PIRATES

Pennsylvania Canal, north of Harrisburg	162
Canal Lock at Harrisburg	146
Vacation party on canal boat *Comfort*	167

	PAGE
Canal in Dauphin Narrows	168
Coming through a Lock	171
Canal Terminus, Columbia	172

HARRISBURG TO THE MARYLAND BORDER

Harrisburg, aerial view	174
River bridges from New Cumberland	176
Steel plant and Steelton from air	178
North from Marsh Run	180
The river at Royalton	182
From Penna. 441 south of Royalton	183
Islands and river from Cly	184
Potholes in river bed, Conewago Falls	185
Upstream from Bainbridge	186
At Billmeyer, showing Railroad Bridge	187
River at Accomac, York County	188
From Chickies Rock, toward Marietta	190
Above Wrightsville, toward Chickies Rock	192
Columbia–Wrightsville Bridge	194
River front at Columbia	195
Long Level panorama	196–197
Turkey Hill from Long Level	198
From Safe Harbor overlook	200
Phoenician (?) "X" stone	202
Wake Robin or Trillium	204
Ferns along fence	205
From Shenk's Ferry	206
McCalls Ferry Bridge (from painting)	208
The Camelback Bridge, east span	209
The Camelback Bridge, west span	210
Sailing above Holtwood Dam	211
York Y.M.C.A. Camp Minqua	212–213
The river at Pequea	215
From lawn of the Tucquan Club	216
Toward the McCalls Ferry gorge	218
Bergamot or Monarda in summer	220
New England Aster, an autumn favorite	221
Toward Holtwood Dam from south	222
Mount Johnson Island, bald eagle sanctuary	225
Peach Bottom, Lancaster County	226
Peach Bottom, York County	227
View from Cutler's Point	228–229

From West Fairview, on the Cumberland County shore opposite Harrisburg, the river scenery is typical of the mid-state Susquehanna — the broad stream, with low tree-clad islands and, in the distance, the Blue Ridge Mountains with V-shaped water gaps.

Photo: R. B. McFarland

PENNSYLVANIA'S SUSQUEHANNA

> The real difficulty in writing of the Susquehanna is the over-richness of the theme. The beauty is varied, as the river flows through mountain passes or placid farmlands, woodland stretches or city parks, embracing islands large and small, washing the base of rocky ledges, flowing rapidly through narrows or idling quietly where it spreads mile-wide from bank to bank. Its history begins earlier than human records. Its fertile shores bred the largest and strongest of all the American natives, and from every country of Europe have come immigrants to make their homes and live on the wealth beside and beneath its waters. Above all and through all, it is the river beloved.
>
> —ALICE R. EATON

SPREADING ACROSS PENNSYLVANIA, like an espaliered tree on a wall, filling the valleys with beauty and sometimes with menace and turmoil, the Susquehanna River drains twenty thousand square miles or almost one-half the area of the Commonwealth. Its eastern tributaries are comparatively short, but some of the sources of the West Branch are so remote from settlements that they are seldom visited even by hunters.

The banks of the main stream, here and there densely populated, are for many miles uninhabited and frequently uninhabitable. The observer looking with wonder upon the Safe Harbor Dam is startled to see a deer almost at his shoulder, venturing from a thicket not far away. The tiny shadow faintly visible upon the unruffled surface of the Holtwood Dam is that of an eagle, whose protected aerie tops a dead tree on the summit of Mount Johnson Island, now almost covered by the backwater of Conowingo Dam. The delicate lines etched on the spring or autumn sky mark a wedge of whistling swan.

The visitor who is acquainted with the past may see another flight against the sky, wholly imaginary—long, broad, apparently black—the incredible multitudes of the passenger pigeon, still remembered by a few, but to most persons almost prehistoric. The farmer scrutinizing an object protruding from a freshet-washed bank stares amazed. Certainly the hard gray substance is not stone! Can these be tusks? Can elephants have ranged in Bradford County?

Not elephants but mastodons, with the curve of their horns measuring twelve feet, and leg bones standing high as a man's shoulder. Perhaps they fed under

Mountain Laurel (*Kalmia latifolia*), State flower of Pennsylvania, is abundant throughout the Susquehanna watershed. In June and early July its masses of pink to white blooms are truly glorious.

Photo: R. B. McFarland

the enormous oaks that left giant descendants first observed by white men three centuries ago. More probably their bodies or bones were carried by ice, which smothered the streams and blanketed the earth.

Long after the mastodon followed the Indian. It is supposed that twenty-five tribes antedated the first for whom we have a name. The name was Andaste; the English when they arrived called them Susquehannocks or Conestogas. Of almost gigantic size, according to Captain John Smith who admired them on the lower river, they lived in palisaded villages scattered through Pennsylvania and Maryland.

Eventually they were subdued by their kinsmen the Iroquois, to whom the whites gave firearms. Their bark houses are dust, blown by the wind; their burial places are ploughed over; time has effaced their picture writings, or the waters of dams have covered them. Into museums are gathered a few of their pestles and mortars, their stone hatchets and war clubs. Three sorts of relics remain abundant—millions of mussel shells where they ate, millions of chips in their quarries, thousands of arrowheads where they pursued game or fought with their enemies.

In a sense, however, the Indians are here. Their paths are our highways or the beds of our railroads. We follow their portages from stream to stream and climb to their lookouts for the refreshment of our spirits. They have named our mountains and streams. The Susquehanna has properly an Indian name that means probably "the long crooked river," and most of its tributaries have Indian names—Lackawanna, Nescopeck, Catawissa, Mahantango, Wyalusing, Meshoppen, Mehoopany, Lycoming, Conodoguinet, Conewago, Conestoga, Pequea, Tucquan.

> "Ye say that all have passed away, the noble and the brave;
> That their light canoes have vanished from off the crystal wave,
> That 'mid the forest where they roamed there rings no hunter's shout,
> But their name is on your waters, ye may not wash it out."

To select any one area of the river as the most beautiful would be folly. The traveler is like a child filling his hands with wild flowers, only to discard them for a more inviting harvest. Here are green meadows, fertile with the silt of ages; there is a mountain split at a right angle. Here, down perpendicular cliffs, course delicate streams; there springs well in caves, or in deep glens in which there is sunlight for only a few hours.

PENNSYLVANIA'S SUSQUEHANNA

From the New York to the Maryland border the river banks are tapestried with bloom. In early spring, against pines and hemlocks with foliage almost black and against bare branches of deciduous trees, the shadbush displays its delicate bloom. Far less known and less admired than it should be, the witch-hazel puts out its yellow flowers from Potter County to York County when all its leaves are gone.

In April, moving north along the river, the American redbud displays its incomparable color. Everywhere on dry wooded hillsides, on banks of culm, laurel sturdily persists, and in moist ravines the evergreen rhododendron abounds, a joy in both summer and winter. On all the hillsides dogwood spreads its cream-white shelves of bloom. The hollows in the southern area are carpeted with mertensia, blue, rose and white all in a single blossom. One observes mournfully a lowland deposit of river coal dust, but is quickly attracted to beds of Dutchman's breeches, exquisite in flower and foliage, of hepatica and anemone. Before May is over, the wild sweet azalea perfumes the forest.

In spring, color is not confined to what children call flowers; there are tiny, brilliant, multitudinous catkins of green and yellow and orange. Before the hardwoods come into leaf, their buds have a delicate color. Alice Meynell speaks of

Photo: J. Horace McFarland Co.

Rhododendron (*R. maximum*) is another outstanding native shrub.

PENNSYLVANIA'S SUSQUEHANNA

Photo: J. Horace McFarland Co.
Hepatica (*H. triloba*)—a herald of spring.

the bouquet of green tulip poplars that the eye may gather in the English woods in the early spring. So it is along the Susquehanna—first a vaguely geometrical figure of misty green; then, pre-eminent for days, a cone of emerald. In the rich bottom lands in late June, fields of wheat, golden rose in their full ripeness, lie between the sapphire river and the azure hillside.

From Harrisburg on a May morning, through a mist of blossoms and young foliage, the river appears to be not a river but a lake, lovely as Maggiore. This broad expanse, like that at Liverpool and at Conejohela, now, alas, prosaically called Long Level, is divided on a day of light clouds and varying winds into fields of rose and jade, mauve and blue. A stronger breeze and the water is suddenly steel, spangled with ripples that catch the light like diamonds.

In autumn the forests bordering the Susquehanna are painted as perhaps are no other American forests. Here are dark hemlock and pine, here white-trunked birches, here yellow-leaved aspens and sycamores, here honey-colored maples, here oaks of all autumn shades. No Vermont road is more dazzling in color than some roads lined by sugar maples in Bedford County where bubble the springs of the Susquehanna's tributary, the Juniata.

In the deep narrow gorge at McCalls Ferry where the width of the river shrinks to a quarter of a mile, the Holtwood Dam holds back the water. Purple shadows fall not alone from the wooded hills, but from unbelievable pyramids of fine coal dredged from the adjacent river bed more than a hundred miles south of the nearest mine.

Riverside beaches, parks and cottage settlements provide playgrounds for thousands. The Harrisburg ball park is on an island in midstream. In canoes and rowboats, sailboats, motorboats and kayaks, youth explores the river and visits its islands. Coal dredges are scattered from Pittston to Holtwood Dam, but no coal dredges can deprive the river of its majesty and beauty. Nor, so far, have engineering operations controlled the mighty power of the floods that avenge the destruction of bordering forests.

At night the river assumes a new loveliness. The stars are reflected and the banks are linked one to the other with gold and silver bands. Miles of street and bridge lights send their beams far out on the water. Lofty bleeder torches gleam against the darkness and wing lights of airplanes fix the source of a deep hum, far overhead. Most spectacular of all bordering areas is Enola where, close to the river, hundreds of locomotives, puffing and groaning, await the signal to depart. Against the columns of black smoke wave plumes of steam, gilded by dazzling headlights.

Looking down upon the Mediterranean, George Santayana declared,

> "Thou carest not what men may tread thy margin;
> Nor I, while from some heather-scented headland
> I may behold thy beauty, the eternal
> Solace of mortals."

Looking down upon Pine Creek flowing a thousand feet below, upon the meeting of the waters at Tioga or Northumberland or Duncannon, or upon the wide expanse of the river at Liverpool or Conejohela, or the man-made lakes behind the Safe Harbor and Conowingo dams, one may apostrophize the Susquehanna and pray that her very different beauty be preserved.

Dr. George Ashley, geologist and lover of the Commonwealth, describes the scenery of Pennsylvania as immensely varied and also "intimate." It lacks, he says, broad plains and great mountain ranges; it possesses little plains, little mountains, little lakes, and waterfalls that make up in variety and number what they lack in size. As though to create a picturesque beauty, the streams often take the hard way through mountains, though wide valleys are at hand.

Photo: J. Horace McFarland Co.
As trees along the river banks begin to show the first traces of spring green, the lower growing Dogwood (*Cornus florida*) makes its display of white in the woods.

Photo: J. Horace McFarland Co.
Mertensia (*M. virginica*) or Virginia Bluebell, a showy spring flower.

Dr. Ashley calls our attention to more than beauty. Why, he asks, does the river cut through the hard mountain when it might wind round its base? Why is this valley broad, that narrow? Why should our Susquehanna once have run north in a bed a hundred feet beneath its present course? How was this deep pit ground out of solid rock? How was this unfathomed bed of sand deposited? Why a plain here and rising terraces there? Why was the river at Marietta once four miles wide?

Scientists have answered these questions. Dr. Ashley in State publications, James MacFarlane in "Coal Regions of America," and many contributors to the journals of scientific and historical associations have described the interesting geology of the river. Recently Dr. Richmond E. Myers in "The Long Crooked River" has given an able account of its history and of those who lived and live along its banks.

In 1840 N. P. Willis published "American Scenery," commenting upon a collection of drawings by William H. Bartlett. In 1872 William Cullen Bryant edited "Picturesque America," two volumes of descriptions and steel engravings to which the term magnificent may well be applied. Both books include pictures

PENNSYLVANIA'S SUSQUEHANNA

of the Susquehanna. In 1948, Mr. Gilbert S. McClintock of Wilkes-Barre collected in "Valley Views of Northeastern Pennsylvania" engravings of paintings of the upper valleys of the Susquehanna, the Lehigh, the Delaware and the Lackawanna. He believes that the present location of many paintings of undoubted interest is unrecorded and unknown.

"Pennsylvania's Susquehanna" is primarily a collection of photographs. The author of the text is indebted to many friends, first of all to Alice R. Eaton of the Harrisburg Public Library, who suggested the preparation of this volume; to the late Dr. J. Horace McFarland, who added his persuasion; to Dr. Elsie Murray, Curator of the Athens, Pennsylvania, Museum, who inherited from her mother, Louise Welles Murray, a deep interest in the river as it flows through northern Pennsylvania, and who is learned in history and science. The articles of Dr. G. F. Dunkelberger of Selinsgrove, of Agnes Selin Schoch of the Selinsgrove *Times* and of Katherine Bennet of the Williamsport Library have all been helpful. No historical society in the length of the river has declined to give aid.

The author is grateful to Nellie Rupley Bergstresser of Selinsgrove, from whose house and garden she has many times watched the river in winter and summer. She will never forget the willingness of Mrs. Bergstresser's boys and girls to follow egrets through a narrow passage between two islands, or to leap out of the canoe when a ridge of ganister appeared to threaten its progress.

She has recorded in the text the names of various persons to whom she is indebted. She would mention also her brother, Paul Singmaster, her chauffeur on many journeys, and other companions—Nina Storrick, Margaret McMillan, Edith Fellenbaum, Dr. George Miksch Sutton, J. Herbert Springer, Dr. and Mrs. Herbert Beck and Dr. and Mrs. Earl Bowen, who on memorable occasions have watched with her the play of afternoon light on Safe Harbor Dam or at Conejohela, or the deepening shadows at Holtwood.

She here acknowledges the patient assistance of her friend Harriet B. Krauth, who is able to reduce the most chaotic of her manuscripts to order.

She is indebted also to one person whom she never saw, her Union grandfather, Edmund Darlington Hoopes of Harford County, Maryland, stationed with his company at the Conowingo Bridge in June, 1863. It was doubtless the family tradition of his service there that first made real to her the name Susquehanna.

From New York State, the North Branch of the Susquehanna enters Pennsylvania. The railroads, here the Erie, have taken full advantage of the paths created by the river. Low hills and a quiet stream are characteristic of the North Branch in the Great Bend section in Susquehanna County.

Photo: *Courtesy The Erie Railroad Co.*

THE NORTH BRANCH

"Hail, charming river! pure transparent flood!
Unstained by noxious swamps or choking mud;
Thundering through broken rocks in whirling foam;
Or pleased o'er beds of glittering sand to roam;
Green be thy banks, sweet forest wandering stream!
Still may thy waves with finny treasures teem;
The silvery shad and salmon crowd thy shores,
Thy tall woods echoing to the sounding oars;
On thy swo'ln bosom floating piles appear,
Filled with the harvest of the rich frontier:
Thy pine-crowned cliffs, thy deep romantic vales,
Where wolves now wander and the panther wails,
Where at long intervals, the hut forlorn
Peeps from the verdure of embowering corn,
In future times (nor distant far the day)
Shall glow with crowded towns and villas gay;
Unnumbered keels thy deepened course divide;
And airy arches pompously bestride;
The domes of Science and Religion rise,
And millions swarm where now a forest lies."

—ALEXANDER WILSON
"The Foresters"

In 1804, Alexander Wilson, an immigrant from Scotland, walked from Gray's Ferry, in the southeast corner of Pennsylvania, to Niagara Falls, in order to observe and sketch American birds. He described his journey in a long poem, "The Foresters." He comments upon the beauty of the Susquehanna and the scarcity of its human inhabitants and foretells the cities on its banks.

FROM NEW YORK STATE into the Commonwealth of Pennsylvania, in what is called the Great Bend, flows the main stream of the Susquehanna's North, sometimes called the East, Branch. Using the valley, as is the way of its kind, enters the Erie Railroad, the startling bray of Diesel engines waking a new echo in the lovely hills. "Wherever a Pennsylvania river breaks through a mountain barrier, there is a railroad to hug its banks." The swift grace of the long trains and the picturesque strength of the stone viaduct crossing Starrucca Creek compensate for the loud blast.

Photos: Courtesy The Erie Railroad Co. and R. B. McFarland

Crossing Starrucca Creek, the Erie Railroad has built a handsome stone viaduct, impressive when seen near at hand, blending with the landscape when viewed from Penna. 92 across the North Branch.

THE NORTH BRANCH

Having bathed the lower slopes of Pennsylvania hills and having been enlarged by Pennsylvania waters, the river, possibly deflected by glacial deposits, returns abruptly to New York State. Leaving Pennsylvania, it does not abandon Susquehanna County, which is its namesake. Entering the county, the traveler must wade or bridge Susquehanna waters. Small streams, originating in tiny lakes, flow either west into Bradford County and the main stream, or east into the Lackawanna and thence into the Susquehanna. Strung together, the names of the lakes make music—Laurel, Quaker and Forest, Elk and Fiddle, Leah and Trip. Lovely Montrose, the county seat, commands the sources of Meshoppen and Wyalusing creeks and thus belongs to the Susquehanna. Other little streams in Bradford and neighboring counties flow from little lakes, a characteristic beauty of the northeast section of the Commonwealth.

The Great Bend has been exploratory; having satisfied itself that Pennsylvania is a good place, the river, after flowing west for forty miles in New York but never more than eight miles distant from Pennsylvania, curves again south. Its course suggests a search for a gateway or the keeping of a tryst. A tryst it is—with the Tioga, originating in Pennsylvania and here called Chemung for the mastodon horns, nine feet from tip to tip, embedded in its banks. Together the two streams turn south.

Their tryst is not immediately consummated. Approaching and separating, they merge at "Te-a-o-ga" or Tioga Point, "the meeting of the waters," whose Indian name was long since changed to Athens in compliment to the intellect of those who settled there. Not only the echoes of high converse linger, but the echoes of song. While a student at the Athens Academy, Stephen Foster wrote his first composition, "Tioga Waltz," for four flutes, dedicated it to a schoolmate and assisted in performing it.

The Point was and is today the beloved subject of artist, photographer and poet. When the hills were still thickly wooded, hills and streams composed a panorama difficult to match in beauty. Charles Miner, a native of Athens long ago, breathed its complaint of neglect and sang its praise.

> "Have not the nymphs of muddy Thames and Seine
> Been covered o'er with wreaths of laurel green?
> Shall my praise warble from no poet's tongue

PENNSYLVANIA'S SUSQUEHANNA

> When Ayr, and Doon, and Tyne, and Ouse are sung?
> Hast not thou often bathed amid my floods,
> And roved delighted thro' my shadowy woods?
> Am I not worthy? view my craggy walls,
> My murmuring ripples, and my thundering falls:
> Green are my meadows, and my hills are high,
> Rich are my fields, and pleasing to the eye;
> Unrivalled flowers deck the banks I love,
> And wide my forests, tall, unequalled, wave."

Today the abode of more than twelve thousand persons and the site of large industries in two towns, Athens and Sayre, the valley presents a new picture.

The river does not at first follow the valleys but cuts through ranges of hills. Inevitably the gap became a gateway not alone for the river and for immense animals of prehistoric ages but for human beings. When the Andastes were conquered and absorbed by their kinsmen, the Iroquois, the valley filled with displaced tribes from the Hudson and Delaware rivers and from the south.

Bound together in a confederation, the six Iroquois Nations spread terror across New York. From west and north they needed to fear no enemy, for they had exterminated their rivals, but at east and south they were vulnerable. In the gap at Tioga Point, they stationed a sachem to pass on all who sought entrance to the Iroquois country.

No post was more important. Here met trails from east and west, here crossed a much-used portage, here was established a famous burial place. Two important highways led south—the Warrior Path and the broadening Susquehanna. Downstream bark canoes and long dugouts swiftly cut the water. Returning, they bore on their prows poles from which floated streamers of hair rooted in patches of flesh and skin. At the Point enemies were tortured, slain or held in captivity.

So far as is known, the first white men to see the lovely Point or any portion of the North Branch, were three Dutch traders who, in 1616, were captured by the Andastes. Held at Tioga because the Indians believed them to be English, they were finally freed and made their way across country to the Delaware River to be picked up by a Dutch ship.

A more important visitor was a young Frenchman, Etienne Brulé, protégé and scout of Champlain. In 1615, he journeyed to Carantouan, a glacial deposit later

Photo: R. B. McFarland

Beyond Oakland in the Great Bend section may be seen this vista of placid river and distant mountains from Penna. 92, which follows the stream.

Re-entering Pennsylvania farther to the west in Bradford County, the North Branch flows past Sayre, here seen from the air. Along the base of the mountain in the distance flows the Chemung River, which joins the North Branch.

Photo: *Courtesy Tioga Point Museum*

mysteriously named Spanish Hill, between Tioga and the New York border, and from there descended the river to Chesapeake Bay, which had been visited by Captain John Smith. Brulé left no record, and there is only a little about him in the record of Champlain.

He journeyed, says Champlain, "along a river that flows in the direction of Florida . . . He continued his course along the river as far as the sea, and to an island and lands near them . . . There was abundance of animals and small game . . . But to traverse these regions required patience, passing extensive wastes . . . The winter was very temperate, it snowed rarely, and when it did the snow was not a foot deep and melted quickly."

Historians, notably Dr. Elsie Murray, have described from present knowledge of the river what Brulé must have seen—the rough crags and wooded hills, the entering streams, the little villages, the Indian lookouts, the evidence of long Indian occupation in the deep ashes of old fires and downstream some pieces of fine pottery.

A hundred years later a different company passed Tioga Point. Poverty-stricken and denied freedom of worship, throngs of Germans and Swiss had gathered along the Rhine, believing mistakenly that they would be welcomed by Queen Anne. From England they had to be sent elsewhere, and after great loss of life en route, several thousand were settled along the Hudson River to manufacture pitch for the Royal Navy. The pine trees proved to be of a species that produced no pitch, and the forlorn Germans emigrated to the Schoharie Creek. Dispossessed of the land that they thought theirs, they decided to move to William Penn's colony, where they felt sure of a welcome.

Crossing to the Susquehanna they descended to Swatara Creek and turned northeast into the present Berks County, where some Germans had already settled. The leader of one migration was a German of extraordinary ability, Conrad Weiser, who had lived with the Mohawks, had learned their language and had been made a member of their nation. Selected by the Iroquois confederation as interpreter and spokesman, he journeyed in the following years back and forth from his home at Womelsdorf to the Indian settlements—Shamokin which is the present Sunbury, Tioga, and the Long House itself near Onondaga, from which the Iroquois governed. Often he was weary and often alarmed lest he be

Photo: R. B. McFarland

The North Branch at Athens. By portaging their canoes at this place, the Indians voyaging upstream avoided a paddle of several miles around Tioga Point.

too late to forestall attack from Indians who were justly enraged by the theft of their lands. Eventually he represented Maryland and Virginia as well as Pennsylvania.

It is our good fortune that Weiser kept careful journals and reported his experiences and reflections in many letters to the Pennsylvania authorities at Philadelphia. In these we read not only the agreements by which he retained the friendship of the Six Nations for the English and the picturesque and to us unpronounceable names of the chiefs who signed the immense parchment documents with their marks and symbols, but vivid descriptions of the rough Susquehanna country through which he so often journeyed in peril of his life. He regarded the Indians along the river, whom he knew so well, with friendliness and in some cases with affection, yet he recognized their fierce bloodthirstiness when roused to indignation by injustice.

Notified in September, 1736, that a delegation from the Six Nations was on

THE NORTH BRANCH

its way to Philadelphia to come to an agreement about lands formerly belonging to the Delawares and still claimed by them, he started from his home in Womelsdorf for Shamokin to meet the chiefs and their companions. Dr. Paul A. W. Wallace in his memorable biography has described their meeting.

When at last the Indians came into view on the broad river that flows here between the forested mountains, Weiser was astonished to see a flotilla of eighteen canoes with a white flag floating in the breeze. For a moment he was dumbfounded; then he did exactly the thing that would please the large delegation—he shook hands with the chiefs, "surrounded by swarms of men, women and children, in blanket cloth mantles and buckskins, some feathered and painted." There were Tocanuntie, Hanickhungo, Tahashwangarorus, Saguchsanyunt, Sawuntga and a host of others: Onondagas, Senecas, Oneidas, Cayugas and Tuscaroras.

Photo: R. B. McFarland

South of Wysox, the river winds in and out among the hills.

Overlooking Tioga Point, south of Athens, where the Chemung River joins the North Branch. In the meadows of the Point, General Sullivan and his army camped during the American Revolution. These waters are the joy of bass fishermen during the season.

Photo: R. B. McFarland

THE NORTH BRANCH

In Philadelphia whither he escorted them, they naturally created a sensation both in the city as they entered, and even more in the Great Meeting House where important conferences were held. "When the Indians came in, treading noiselessly on sepacs or moccasins, and took their seats, their brown faces, some painted with streaks of cinnabar or vermilion, and the red and blue blankets which they wore thrown loosely over the shoulder and kept to the body with the left hand, threw a splash of rich color against the thinner, sharper tints of city faces and city costumes."

With dignity and solemnity, according to their fashion, they presented their gifts, among them a beaver coat and bundles of skins brought down from the upper Susquehanna. They uttered the solemn cry with which they set their seal of approbation on their deeds. This cry, which must have echoed innumerable times across the Susquehanna, is described by Weiser.

"When any Proposals are made by them in their Treaties with the white People, or by the white People to them, they make the Io-hau, or Shout of Approbation, which is performed thus: The Speaker after a Pause, in a slow Tone pronounces the U . . . huy; all the other Sachems in perfect silence; so soon as he stops, they all with one voice, in exact Time, begin one general Io, raising and falling their Voices as the Arch of a Circle, and then raise it as high as at first, and stop at the Height at once, in exact time, and if it is of great Consequence, the Speaker gives the U . . . huy thrice, and they make the Shout as often. It is usual, when the white People speak to them, and they give a Belt or String of Wampum, for the Interpreter to begin the U . . . huy, and the Indians make the Shout."

When they returned home by way of Womelsdorf, they had deeded to the English "all the said River Susquehannah, with the Lands lying on both sides thereof, to Extend Eastward as far as the heads of the Branches or Springs which run into the said Susquehannah, and all the lands lying on the West side of the said River to the setting of the Sun, and to extend from the mouth of the said River Northward, up the same to the Hills or mountains called in the language of the said Nations, the Tyannuntasacta, or Endless hills, and by the Delaware Indians, the Kekkachtanin Hills."

In the Capitol at Harrisburg in sight of the Susquehanna these great documents are preserved and are at times displayed. Some visitors pass them with only a glance. Others pore over the long names and the tiny crude pictures of birds and animals that serve as signatures.

In 1736 Governor Gooch of Virginia requested the Six Nations to send delegates to a council in Philadelphia, and Weiser offered his service as messenger. Because of bad weather and flooded streams, he was not able to start till the end of February, 1737. He kept two journals, one in English for the authorities at Philadelphia, the other in German for his family.

Leaving the inhabited part of Pennsylvania, and accompanied by a guide and also by an Indian who had been long sick at his house, he crossed the Endless Mountains. Snow covered the ice on the steep slopes. In the tiny village at Shamokin no one was at home and only after several days was he able to attract the attention of an Indian in a hut across the Susquehanna, which was filled with floating ice. In a small canoe they made the dangerous crossing.

Following the West Branch, they reached Shikellamy's town and after some days welcomed his return. The waters had again risen; weak from starvation, they forded the deep and icy streams. "The 22d we came to a village called Ostuaga, from a high rock which lies opposite. However, before we came in sight of the village, we reached a large creek, which looked more dreadful than the one of yesterday. After repeated firing of our guns, two young Indians came from the village to see what was to be done. They brought, at our request, a canoe from the village, and took us across. We quartered ourselves with Madam Montour, a French woman by birth, of a good family, but now in mode of life a complete Indian. She treated us very well according to her means, but had very little to spare this time, or, perhaps, dared not let it be seen, on account of so many hungry Indians about. She several times in secret gave me and Stoffel as much as we could eat, which had not happened to us before for ten days; she showed great compassion for us, saying that none of the Indians where we were going had anything to eat, except the Onontagers, which my Indian fellow-travellers refused to believe, until we found it true by experience."

Beyond, the messengers traversed a deep valley, then clambered along the precipitous bank, chopping footholds in the ice as they went. Presently to avoid the frequent wading of an icy creek called by the Indians "Lost" or

Photo: R. B. McFarland

From a hill on US 220–309 north of Towanda, county seat of Bradford County, the North Branch is seen winding through upland farm country. In late summer many fields are white with buckwheat bloom.

Photo: R. B. McFarland

Standing Stone, Ossinepachte to the Indian, is a rock projecting twenty-four feet above the water, embedded by a glacier in the west bank of the North Branch near the site of Asylum. It can be best reached by boat from one of the nearby small settlements.

THE NORTH BRANCH

"Bewildered," they determined to try the mountainside. Here, says Weiser, Shikellamy "caught hold of a flat stone, sticking in the root of a fallen tree, which came loose, and his feet slipping from under him, he fell at a place which was steeper than the roof of a house. He could not catch hold of anything, but continued slipping on the snow and ice for about three rods, when his pack, which he carried in Indian fashion, with a strap around his breast, passed on one side of a sapling and he on the other, so that he remained hanging by the strap until we could give him assistance. If he had slipped half a rod farther he would have fallen over a precipice about one hundred feet high, upon other craggy rocks. I was two steps from him when he fell. We were all filled with horror, but were obliged to proceed until we reached a place where we could descend into the valley, which did not take place for a quarter of an hour. When we reached the valley Shikellamy looked around at the height of the precipice on which he had fallen. We looked at him: he stood still in astonishment, and said: 'I thank the great Lord and Creator of the world, that he had mercy on me, and wished me to continue to live longer.'"

Crossing the icy stream again and again in water to their waists, they slept, as ever hungry, in a hut made of spruce boughs. They came upon a "wonder of nature," a stream dividing against a linden tree into two streams, one flowing south into a branch, the other into the main stream, a division of the waters that Dr. Wallace has verified. When they reached a white oak grove in which the snow had disappeared, they felt as though they "had escaped from hell."

Fed by an old squaw "whose skin was like bark and whose fingernails were like eagle's claws," they passed on toward Onondaga and the conference with the Indians, through country with which Weiser had been familiar in his youth.

The journey home was far less perilous, since the river was swollen by melted snow. Devising bark canoes, they made swift progress. The conference had been successful—peace with Virginia was assured and Weiser composed the last sentence in his vivid record:

"Honour and praise, power and glory be given to Almighty God forever and ever."

Weiser served as guide to Lewis Evans, maker of maps, on his surveying trip up the Susquehanna, to Count von Zinzendorf, the Moravian, hungry for souls.

Near Rummerfield an attractive overlook along US 6-309 shows, in a bend of the North Branch, the site of Asylum, planned as a refuge for Queen Marie Antoinette and the Dauphin of France from the horrors of the French Revolution. Today the site is lovely, peaceful farmland.

Photo: Courtesy Penna. Dept. of Highways

THE NORTH BRANCH

to John Bartram, the botanist, delighted by lovely new plants. Together Weiser, Evans and Bartram crossed the river and its branches, together pressed through thickets of laurel and rhododendron, together made their beds under towering pine trees of a height Bartram estimated but refused to report because he thought no one would believe him.

After General Braddock was defeated in 1755, the Indians, resenting the theft of their land and incited and sometimes accompanied by the French, attacked the long line of English and German settlements in Pennsylvania, torturing and murdering the colonists and setting aflame their cabins. Among those "captivated" or destroyed were Susanna Nitschman, a young Moravian, who in Tioga suffered torture of the body and worse torture of the soul until she died, and Frances Slocum from Wilkes-Barre, traced by her family after many years had made of her an Indian in feeling and instinct. From a far southern Susquehanna tributary Mary Jemison was carried west, then north.

More unnatural conflicts, called the Pennamite Wars, stained the river. The original charter of Connecticut specified an area extending from sea to sea. Later the King presented some of the same land to William Penn, and for almost a century Connecticut did not remember that the northern half of what is now Pennsylvania was hers. Learning of its beauty and fertility, a land company first explored, then sent two hundred families to settle in the Wyoming Valley, extending from the present Pittston to the present Nanticoke. Surrounded by mountains that rise to nineteen hundred feet, with broad, fertile bottom land, the valley seemed a paradise.

Promptly the Delawares, who had lost their own lands and had settled in the valley, massacred some of the whites and drove the others away. In a few years forty Connecticut men, led by Captain Zebulon Butler, built a blockhouse and stockade called Forty Fort, to be promptly assailed by two hundred Pennsylvanians armed with a cannon. Five times the Yankees returned and five times were driven off. A truce was called during the Revolution, and after further strife the matter was adjudicated in 1800.

The Revolution was fought not only on or near the eastern seacoast and the Canadian boundary but as fiercely along the Susquehanna. In 1778, Colonel John Butler led a large force of British and Indians south to the Wyoming Valley.

Wyalusing Rocks, high above the North Branch along US 6–309, served the Indians as a lookout point for the Wyalusing Path, a trail running from Muncy on the West Branch of the Susquehanna.

Photo: Courtesy Penna. Dept. of Highways

THE NORTH BRANCH

At once Yankees and Pennsylvanians joined forces in self-defense. Largely outnumbered, partly because their men were fighting in the Continental Army, they soon realized their helplessness. Fleeing eastward, women and children wandered in a dismal swamp, called thereafter The Shades of Death. "Queen" Esther Montour, a half-breed hitherto friendly, with her own hand brained fifteen captives on a rock near the river, according to Indian ethics a just equivalent for her son, whom the English had killed.

The whites did not go long unavenged. Moving northward from Fort Muncy on the West Branch of the river, Colonel Thomas Hartley sped toward quickly abandoned Indian Sheshequin Town and Queen Esther's Town, then on to Tioga. Having collected captives and plunder, the soldiers ran, torch in hand, from bark house to bark house and from one harvest field to another until news of a numerous British force turned them back.

The British continued to incite the Indians to destruction and murder, and from Indian gardens and fields supplies continued to pour to the British in New York and Fort Niagara. Realizing the menace to the American cause, the Congress and General Washington directed General John Sullivan to march his army from Easton to the Susquehanna and from there northward. At Wilkes-Barre he loaded some of his supplies in boats constructed in far-away Middletown or Marietta below John Harris' ferry and poled or rowed up the river, parallel to the course of his pack horses on the bank.

Tioga Point was the scene of extraordinary preparations and of a unique rendezvous. General George Clinton separated himself from the forces watching the British in New York City and marched to Lake Otsego, source of the large arm of the North Branch. Drought prevailed and the river was too low for travel; but while rafts were being constructed, sappers easily dammed the narrow outlet of the lake. Higher and higher rose the water; when at last it was released, the watching Indians saw a terrifying miracle. Riding the flood, Clinton and his troops floated down to Tioga to join General Sullivan.

Northwest from their base, well equipped, alert for ambush, fighting one small battle, setting fire to villages and crops, Sullivan led the combined forces. When at last he turned back, his men had burned two hundred thousand bushels of corn and destroyed forever the power of the Long House.

PENNSYLVANIA'S SUSQUEHANNA

South of Tioga Point, past the long-abandoned sites of Queen Esther's Town and Sheshequin Town, between broad fields of grain, the river continues for about fifteen miles in an almost straight line. Before it passes Towanda, it begins to flow in deep valleys. Its lovely curves, paralleled by wooded hills, suggest a creature ever looking backward at its own beauty. Perhaps it is excited by the approach of the lively Towanda, the Wysox, the Wyalusing, the Little Tuscarora, the Mehoopany, the Tunkhannock, or perhaps foresees the moment when, joined from the northeast by the Lackawanna, it will of necessity broaden and deepen to calmness and sobriety.

Always there are mountains in view. In 1799, Isaac Weld, Jr., published a description of this section of the Susquehanna in his account of his travels in North America.

"The Country is extremely uneven and rugged; indeed, from Lochartzburgh (Athens) till within a short distance of Wilkes-Barre, it is bounded the entire way

Photo: R. B. McFarland

South of Wyalusing on US 6–309, well-tilled fields border the river.

30

THE NORTH BRANCH

Photo: Courtesy The Rev. and Mrs. Elmer Truches
This giant elm (*Ulmus americana*), along the shores of the North Branch near Laceyville, has seen generations of red and white men come and go.

by steep mountains on one side or the other. The mountains are never to be met with at both sides of the same part of the river, except it be at places where the river takes a very sudden bend; but whenever you perceive a range of mountains on one side, you are sure to find an extensive plain on the opposite one; scarcely in any part do the mountains extend for more than one mile together on the same side of the river, and in many instances, during the course of one mile, you will perceive more than a dozen different changes of the mountains from one side to the other . . . At every bend the prospect varies, and there is scarcely a spot between Lochartzburg and Wilkes-Barre where the painter would not find subjects."

Photo: R. B. McFarland

Some of the loveliest river views may be seen from the river bridges, as at Tunkhannock where US 309 crosses the North Branch.

THE NORTH BRANCH

The curves of the river below Towanda are those of a child's game, "Go in and out the windows"—out at Wysox, in above Standing Stone, out at the mouth of Rummerfield Creek. The Standing Stone, a great slab sixteen feet broad and four feet through, embedded in the river and projecting twenty-four feet, reminds the observer of the mighty power of the glacier that ages ago moved southward. On the creek called by his name, Anthony Rummerfield built a sawmill, and opposite at the mouth of Durell Creek Stephen Durell built another. Here began the enormous lumber business of northeastern Pennsylvania. It was estimated that in 1849, in less than a month a hundred million feet were floated down the North Branch.

High on the east bank runs the Sullivan Trail, from which one may look upon a vast bow of the river, across cultivated land and beyond to wooded hills. Visible through the binocular glasses provided by the State Highway Department stands a white shaft, dwarfed by the distance. Here lay Asylum, the refuge prepared in 1793 by loyal Frenchmen for Marie Antoinette and her son. A granite boulder marks the site of the market place; nearby stood the log house built for the Queen, tiny when compared with the palaces that had been her home but large in comparison with other dwellings in the settlement.

After the King had been executed, the Queen and the Dauphin lay in prison. Long-accumulated resentment against tyranny and waste and distrust of the Queen swelled into demands for revenge upon the royal family and the nobility. Their property seized, their lives endangered, the nobles began to flee. Many had friends in the United States, where French aid had been the turning point in the struggle for liberty. General Lafayette had been imprisoned, but others could be assisted.

Among the fugitives, Omer Talon, who had been the King's Advocate, had taken ship for England and later for Philadelphia, safely if uncomfortably concealed in a wine-cask. Another was Louis de Noailles, brother-in-law of Lafayette, who had been assigned to receive at Yorktown in 1781 the surrendered sword of General Cornwallis. Amply supplied with funds, these and other Frenchmen opened a house in Philadelphia, both for refugees from France and for survivors of the massacre of San Domingo.

PENNSYLVANIA'S SUSQUEHANNA

In Philadelphia they were too near the sea; their secret and important plans required a remote refuge. Contracting for land with Robert Morris and John Nicholson, who owned an immense tract in northeastern Pennsylvania, they prepared to settle along the Susquehanna. The leaders in the enterprise journeyed by wagon roads, then by bridle paths and boats. In their company were military men, former priests, scientists and others of fame and ability.

The majestic trees on the hillsides and the rich grass in the bottom land showed that they had selected well. Determined to make up by courage and industry for lack of experience, they built houses and laid out gardens. A hundred and eighty years after Etienne Brulé had journeyed down the Susquehanna, the curving river and the bordering hills heard smooth, musical French. Since their needs had to be supplied from Philadelphia, Wilkes-Barre or Tioga Point, it was necessary to add patience to other virtues.

Joyfully they erected a house for the Queen; waiting, they were at first gay, then merely cheerful. Soon their cheerfulness was forced. They watched for the long heavy Durham boats that should bring the Queen and her son and their attendants—why did they not come?

Their watching was vain; before the lovingly built "Queen's house" was finished, the Queen had been executed and the young Dauphin had vanished forever. Other famous men arrived and for a while became a part of the colony. When the fierce storm of revolution had spent its fury, some of the visitors returned to France and others joined their friends in England. Only a few remained in America. The Queen's house was taken down for the sake of safety. Years later when records were studied, not alone of France and the United States but from the museums of Pennsylvania and Tioga Point, the settlements were made to rise again, at any rate in the imagination of those who value courage in misfortune. Writers of romance at least have heard spinets tinkle, violins wail and French ladies laugh their light happy laughter.

Below Rummerfield, the Sullivan Trail, tracing the route of General Sullivan's army, continues high above the river, opening one lovely vista of grazing land after the other, and in the distance range after range of wooded and hazy mountains.

Wyalusing Rocks command the scene of even more courageous adventure than

Photo: R. B. McFarland

South of Tunkhannock, Penna. 92 branches from US 6 at Osterhout and follows the stream to the southeast. Along this route are many delightful vistas of the North Branch, as here, south of Falls.

Photo: R. B. McFarland

Campbell's Ledge, a high outcrop of rock near the confluence of the Lackawanna River, was another Indian lookout of bygone days. Here the Susquehanna reaches its "farthest east."

Asylum. The names that float upon the air are not those of French aristocrats but of German Moravians, on missionary journeys. With heroic effort and patience, they won a few converts. They founded a village that they called Friedenshutten or Huts of Peace; here, they reported, prevailed "order, industry and harmony." From the belfry of a little church sounded the call to prayer; in a little schoolhouse children and adults were taught to read their own Delaware language and to understand German. Corn was cultivated in fenced-in fields, berries and wild fruits were to be had for the gathering, sugar maples were plentiful and game was abundant.

The Delawares had been promised perpetual possession, but their overlords, the Iroquois, sold their land. The Delawares appealed to Governor Penn in vain, and mournfully the converts departed under the leadership of the Moravian Bishop Ettwein. Carrying their church bell, they set out on a torturing journey through swamps and forests to Ohio. A hundred years later the site of Friedenshutten was located by historians and a monument erected.

THE NORTH BRANCH

From the highway one sees walls of trees and their massed, indistinguishable summits but not certain great survivors of the past. Below Skinner's Eddy, where the river winds into Wyoming County, stands a mammoth elm that seems properly to belong to the age of the mastodon. Its owner has spared no pains to extend its life. Its height is estimated to be three hundred feet, the spread of its crown three hundred, the circumference of its trunk thirty. If there is a slight understatement in its supposed age of three hundred years, it might easily have waved its delicate leaves over Brulé and his companions. When the Connecticut men came to view the King's grant, it was a large tree; the French seeking their Asylum passed under its spreading branches. Ardent missionaries, Indians trying to hold their streams and forests, soldiers on punitive raids—all must have welcomed its shade. In 1949 youthful representatives of the National Geographic Society contemplated it with awe and recorded for the world the majestic spread of its boughs.

Photo: R. B. McFarland

North Branch Susquehanna River showing Pittston and river bridge from West Pittston.

37

Wilkes-Barre, in the heart of the anthracite coal region, is the principal city of the North Branch as well as the county seat of Luzerne County. From the air the relation of the city and the Susquehanna is clearly seen.

Photo: *Ace Hoffman Studios*

THE NORTH BRANCH

At Meshoppen the Sullivan Trail leaves the river to its winding course, now east, now south, now directly north, now south once more. The traveler cannot visit all the river's tributaries, but reaching Tunkhannock Creek he should turn aside. A good road follows the lovely stream, and a dozen miles away, at Nicholson, the concrete viaduct of the Delaware and Lackawanna Railroad, largest of its kind in the world, rises two hundred and forty feet above the floor of the valley.

Pretty Tunkhannock, against its backdrop of Mount Avery, seems to say, "Here, sit thee down!" Alas, too many roads invite! To follow the river to the south one should select Route 92, which shares the deep valley with the Lehigh Valley Railroad. On each side are hills, apparently too steep to have suffered the removal of their forests. Traffic seems to prefer other highways, and one may drive slowly or halt entirely without endangering life.

At Falls the highway crosses to the west side of the river, and soon the eye of the geologist is rewarded by the remaining sand of a long delta, a deposit probably concerned with the origin of the Wyoming Valley. In late June the eye of the botanist catches the glorious red fruits of a few bushes of *Sambucus pubens*, the red-berried elderberry, far enough below the road to be safe from destruction.

Its curves less bold, its current less rapid, the river cuts through the mountains out of Wyoming County and into the Wyoming Valley, which was filled, ages before the time of man, with a strange tropical growth. Thick mist darkened the air, tall ferns formed rank forests, tremendous vines draped the giant trees. Presently over all flowed the waters of an inland sea. The mammoth trunks rotted and sank and layers of vegetation mounted one upon another, all eventually to be buried under the immense weight of shifting rock, which pressed from them all but their one indestructible element, the carbon that had given them body and form and sometimes recorded even the shape and design of delicate leaves.

Again the scene changed, the hills lifted, and ice moved down from the north in a thick layer. Covering northeast Pennsylvania it sometimes advanced, sometimes receded, deepening the valleys, leveling mountain ranges, shearing the sloping sides of mountains. At last the ice sheet melted and the water drained away. Through centuries summer followed spring, then the rich foliage was colored by tints of autumn. Brown or copper-colored men, tribe after tribe, followed the valley or looked down from the hilltops, each believing the land his own.

Photo: R. B. McFarland

The North Branch at Wilkes-Barre from dike south of business section, showing river bridge and buildings in center of city.

The war cries of Indians battling with one another, the outcries of tortured victims, the loud disputes of men of the same Anglo-Saxon blood over land have long since died away. The tears of the captives, Frances Slocum and Susanna Nitschman, are dried. The laughter of Sullivan's boatmen, the pad of his pack horses, the shouts of his assembling soldiers are heard no more. A few outcries, and silence and beauty prevailed. Gradually they were succeeded by clamor and ugliness and the muffled groans of a new sort of tragedy.

Below rock-striped Campbell's Ledge, the river turns at a right angle and makes its way through the broad-floored valley in a southwesterly direction. At Pittston, named for the English statesman always friendly to the American colonies, enters the Lackawanna, not nearly so large as the tributaries presently flowing in from the west, but of great importance and fame.

Beginning at the present Carbondale, extending to Pittston and down to Nanticoke where the Wyoming Valley ends, a distance of forty-six miles, then

THE NORTH BRANCH

southeastward into Schuylkill and Carbon counties, lay the tropical forest, pressed upon by shifting rock until it was transformed into anthracite, hardest and most valuable of all varieties of coal. Some beds measured a mere inch in thickness, some a hundred feet. Some remained horizontal, others shifted and bent under moving strata. Some lay fourteen hundred feet below sea level, some fourteen hundred feet above. Some etched on the surface of the earth black lines with a nature and value long unsuspected. It is estimated that more than twenty million tons awaited the uses of mankind.

Slowly men came to discover that the black rock could be ignited. Before Connecticut men and Pennsylvanians fought for the valley and General Sullivan led his force upstream, coal was burned in a forge in Wilkes-Barre. The first shallow mine was opened at Carbondale in 1822, and its product shipped by sled and raft.

Like frantic moles, men began to bore downward and tunnel forward and back

Coal breaker along the North Branch at Plymouth.

Photo: R. B. McFarland

PENNSYLVANIA'S SUSQUEHANNA

and to right and left. Lighted only by the lamps in their caps, the feeble gleam of which was lost a few feet away, those who lived on farms or in forests in the blessed light of day must have been appalled to descend into the ebon blackness. When two miners working together ceased to speak or to wield picks and shovels, the silence was that of death. In certain areas they must have been ever conscious that above their heads lay the whole weight of the flowing river.

Experienced miners arrived from across the Atlantic—English, Welsh and Irish, escaping, they believed, from too long hours and too small wages. Into the earth plunged deeper shafts; from them on ever-deepening levels spread a maze of tunnels, ceiled and walled by coal, traversed by tracks on which first men or mules, then electric power moved the coal to hoists that lifted it to the surface.

Boats transported the coal on the Susquehanna and its tributaries, then on

Photo: R. B. McFarland

Tilsbury's Knob, overlooking West Nanticoke on US 11, gets its name from an interesting tale of an early settler.

Photo: R. B. McFarland

From the bridge carrying Penna. 29 from Shickshinny to Mocanaqua is a charming North Branch view as the river turns south.

parallel canals. Before many years railroads entering through gaps in the hills flung bridges across the river, first of wood, then of iron, then of steel and concrete. Activity was continuous. In the mines day and night did not alternate; night and men's labor never ceased.

Beside the river towered lofty, many-windowed frame buildings called breakers. Lifted to the summits of the breakers, the coal moved downward in slanting chutes, and on boards placed across the chutes sat boys and old men. Damming the coal with their feet, they held it until they had picked out what pieces of slate and other impurities they could seize in the brief moment until the dark, ever-moving stream passed to the next pocket.

Dust and fine coal blackened the river and formed mountainous heaps along its banks. The houses remained unpainted, for paint was a waste of money where coal dust filled the air. Little streams were dyed yellow with sulphur. Where rock was left insufficiently supported, cave-ins pitted the earth, occasionally engulfing buildings. Some of the huge breakers, unrepaired as the supply of coal dwindled, swayed visibly in the wind. Would not the next blast send them crashing to earth?

The imagination, not wholly unwilling to dwell on the horrors of war and massacre in the lovely valley and to find a sort of thrill even in the Shades of Death, shudders to share in the vigil of mothers, sweethearts and wives at the head of a mine shaft. The mammoth pumps, removing nine tons of air and ten tons of water for each ton of coal, may fail. Lethal gas may seep through tunnels, or falls of rock or coal choke the entrance until all behind the barriers are starved. Sometimes greed or error has robbed the ceilings of support while mines were still being operated.

At the northern gate of the Wyoming Valley, in what is called the Twin Shaft disaster, the river itself became one of the ministers of death. A hundred miners perished when a collapsed roof created a funnel for the plunging torrent. At Avondale near the lower end of the valley another hundred met a less merciful fate when fire destroyed both hoist and ventilating apparatus at the single exit.

Each disaster inspired the composers of ballads to set simple words to mournful tunes. A bard of Avondale sang the praises of two would-be rescuers:

> "Two Welshmen brave, without dismay,
> And courage without fail
> Went down the shaft without delay,
> In the mines of Avondale."

Scores of similar dirges have floated above the river, commemorating favorably the heroes of the mining country and denouncing others who were justly or unjustly blamed for the disasters. However gay the "collier lad" appeared to be, his good spirits must often have been assumed.

> "I'm a jovial collier lad, and blithe as blithe can be,
> For let the times be good or bad, they're all the same to me.
> 'Tis little of the world I know, and care less for its ways
> For where the dog-star never glows, I wear away my days.

> "At every shift, be't soon or late, I haste my bread to earn,
> And anxiously my kindred wait and watch for my return,
> For death, that levels all alike, whate'er their rank may be,
> Amid the fire and damp may strike, and fling his darts at me."

Photo: Courtesy Penna. Dept. of Forests and Waters

A worthwhile side trip from Shickshinny on US 11 is to Ricketts Glen State Park. In this primeval glen, along Kitchen Creek, is a series of cascades along the creek as Harrison Wright Falls above, descending the side of North Mountain.

Wapwallopen is situated on a bluff where the North Branch, having turned south at Shickshinny, bends abruptly west. Looking north from Penna. 29, the motorist enjoys this delightful river view.

Photo: R. B. McFarland

THE NORTH BRANCH

Gradually, because of the awakening of public conscience, the improvement of safety inventions and the demands of miners, conditions improved. Fatalities have not been out of proportion to the enormous work accomplished. In 1870 there were fifteen deaths in the mining of a million tons of coal; in 1947 there were three.

Each decade brought new races to make their homes in the Lackawanna or Susquehanna valleys. English, Welsh and Irish miners were followed by Slavs and Italians. Beside the right-angled cross of the Roman Catholic and Protestant rose the bulbous tower of the Orthodox Greek Catholic and the three-armed cross of the Ruthenian. Picturesque costumes and picturesque ways long enlivened the streets of adjacent cities and villages.

Not all the coal region is grimy and unsightly. There are dilapidated villages, but there are also handsome cities and towns. Scranton is the third largest city in Pennsylvania. There is no longer sufficient work in the mines for the male population, and occupation is required for their large families. Here where coal produces cheap power are numerous factories that manufacture lace, silk, rayon, furniture, mining machinery, shoes and various other products.

The Scranton International Correspondence School, begun for the training of young miners in their dangerous craft, is now one of the large educational institutions of the world, with instruction covering many fields. In the city are an Art Gallery and a Museum of Natural History, a Roman Catholic university and a Roman Catholic college for women. The descendants of those whose hands were grained till they died with the grime of the mine or the breaker have opportunities of which no "breaker-boy" or mule-driver dreamed.

The landscape is by no means unlovely. At night the moon faintly silvers the culm banks. On the hillside blooms the pink and white laurel, and here and there small birch groves gaily take the breeze. To east and west are forests and waterfalls, to the north the little lakes of Susquehanna and Bradford counties shine in the sun. A family with a car or with bus-fare or a boy or girl with a bicycle has beauty at hand.

Charles Miner described in prose as well as poetry the once romantic beauty of the Wyoming Valley:

"It is diversified by hill and dale, uplands and intervale. Its character of extreme richness is derived from the extensive flats, or river bottoms, which, in some places, extend from one to two miles from the stream, unrivaled in expansive

Photo: R. B. McFarland
From East Bloomsburg a long, straight stretch of river bisects a wide valley.

beauty, unsurpassed in luxuriant fertility. Though now generally cleared and cultivated, to protect the soil from floods a fringe of trees is left along each bank of the river—the sycamore, the elm, and more especially the black walnut, while here and there, scattered through the fields, a huge shell-bark yields its summer shade to the weary laborers, and its autumn fruit to the black and gray squirrel. Pure streams of water come leaping from the mountains, imparting health and pleasure in their course; all of them abounding with the delicious trout. Along those brooks and in the swales, scattered through the uplands, grow the wild plum and butter-nut, while, wherever the hand of the white man has spared it, the native grape may be gathered in unlimited profusion. I have seen a grape-vine bending beneath its purple clusters, one branch climbing a butter-nut, loaded with fruit, another branch resting upon a wild plum, red with its delicious burden; the while, growing in the shade, the hazel-nut was ripening its rounded kernel.

"Such were the common scenes when the white man first came to Wyoming.

THE NORTH BRANCH

Game of every sort was abundant. The quail whistled in the meadow; the pheasant rustled in its leafy covert; the wild duck reared her brood and bent the reed in every inlet; the red deer fed upon the hills; while in the deep forests, within a few hours' walk, was found the stately elk. The river yielded at all seasons a supply of fish; the yellow perch, the pike, the catfish, the bass, the roach, and, in the spring season, myriads of shad."

Today the valley is changed, but still light and shade combine and alternate in mysterious grandeur. Looking south on an August morning, one longs to fix on canvas the rising mists, the fleece-like steam, the dark streamers of smoke, cut by shafts of golden sunlight. The river, however, coal-stained, coursing from side to side, appears most of the time to be blue.

One's first impression of the valley is not only of spectacular beauty but of prosperity and constant activity. Handsome bridges span the river; the streets

Photo: R. B. McFarland
Blue Hill rising above Riverside, opposite Danville, accents the view from the Danville river front.

A ridge road from Danville reaches Sunbury, where from Mile Hill is seen the North Branch and the lower valley of the sister river, the West Branch of the Susquehanna.

Photo: R. B. McFarland

THE NORTH BRANCH

through which one traverses Wyoming, Kingston and Plymouth are wide and tree-shaded. Civic pride expresses itself in churches, schools and libraries; varied industries promise opportunity to the diligent and ambitious. State markers remind us that yonder the brave Connecticut men built their Forty Fort and that there along the river Queen Esther avenged the death of her son.

On the east bank lies Wilkes-Barre. Founded by Connecticut men, it was named for John Wilkes and Isaac Barré, English friends of the American colonists. Once prosperous because of its coal, it is now prosperous because of many other industries. Parks offer entertainment to children and adults, lakes invite to uplands. Not far away flows Kitchen Creek with its magic of forests and waterfalls.

At Nanticoke, out at last from the narrowing valley, the river leaves barely enough space for the highway and two railroads. As trucks and trains thunder past, one seems to be in a coal and freight chute. The town runs uphill, and here live and work ten thousand miners. In Shickshinny, thus named by the Indians because of its five mountain spurs, a steeply rising foundation, all that remains of a ruined colliery, recalls a hill town in Italy. Here, as in a thousand places, one should view the river both up and downstream.

The tributaries of the river have been black; now they flow more nearly clear. Coal, however, is still present. Salvaged in large quantities, it is deposited in pyramids nearby or carried sometimes high in air to the buyers' trucks. As the water deepens, dredges trail across its surface. Since 1889 a yearly average of seven hundred and fifty thousand tons has been lifted from the bottom.

In a broad valley, eastward to Wapwallopen, against the shoulder of a lovely hill that served as an Indian lookout, then southwest to Berwick, the island-dotted river ambles on. At Berwick, the American Car and Foundry Company spreads its neat shops over almost seven hundred acres. Bloomsburg and Danville are famous for State institutions established in commanding positions, one a teachers' college, the other a hospital.

Since it was joined by the Lackawanna at Pittston, the North Branch, which has coursed through Pennsylvania for about two hundred miles, has been swelled by many creeks—Harvey, the outlet of lovely Harvey Lake, Hemlock, Shickshinny, Wapwallopen, Fishing, Catawissa. A little farther on it will receive its largest tributary, the West Branch, once rich in treasure, still rich in beauty.

Near Cherry Tree on the West Branch headwaters, Indians hid their canoes and crossed the mountains on foot to streams flowing west.

Photo: R. B. McFarland

THE WEST BRANCH

"Futile to try naming the leaf shades: spring tints of sea and air, silver-grays, blue-violet, yellow-green and so on. Note how the better landscape painters shy from the hightoned autumn scene. Old gold of the hickories, never two alike nor coming out together, more featureful because of growing scarcity in the East. Fire cherry early, late black cherry and tulip bravely turning when the mind may be sombered by the general dulling. Hollow apple tree homely leaved but with fruit clinging and covering ground under, scarlet ivy running inside and along the lower limbs. The basswood's yellow-orange spotting. Delicate green sycamore with decoration enough in the bark, yet whose every leaf tries to carry the tinge of all rivals. Ubiquitous sumac gala, clothing ugly waste spaces and waving varicolored fronds from June to November, scorning science and season, meliorating the too solid green of midsummer.

"When the maple parade is passing, these and scores of minors in hollow and fence-row take over the exhibit, to cheer and enlighten through weeks of early frost and storm. The vegetable dies more graciously than the animal—fragrance and artistry to the last.

"My autumn favorite is the ash, rarely mentioned, now coming in more along fences, on road banks, in old field edges and sprout forest; colors unnamable precisely, indeterminate shades of bronze, gun metal, purple, cherry, blue-green, violet —through the gamut that seems to say—you are overdone with red and yellow, I will stay with you in art and dress motive through all urban glares and winters."

—FREDERIC BRUSH
"Walk the Long Years," 1946

THE HISTORY OF MANY MILES of the North Branch of the Susquehanna may be read on roadside markers, in towering collieries, in manufacturing plants, in towns and cities. The story of the West Branch, called by the Indians Otzinachson, is not so well recorded; there are in comparison only a few roadside signs and a few cities and towns. Over long spaces in its two-hundred-mile course, there are no human habitations. It disappears into deep gorges so that to trace its blue ribbon one must climb mountains or struggle through thickets.

Its source illustrates a fact that is a commonplace to the geographer but startles the unthinking observer. Through Cambria, Clearfield and Indiana counties where it rises, runs the divide between two watersheds, and springs emptying into Chesapeake Bay neighbor those flowing into the Gulf of Mexico. Raindrops, blown this way or that by varying winds, may be carried north, south, east or west.

PENNSYLVANIA'S SUSQUEHANNA

Between its springs and its junction with the North Branch at Northumberland the river makes its way through wide and fertile lowlands, cuts through mountain ridges or washes the bases of precipitous cliffs. Its fall measures at times four hundred feet to the mile.

Along its banks grow hundreds of varieties of plants, from infinitesimal mosses that coat the gray rocks with emerald, and tiny houstonia that dapples the meadows, to soaring pines and hemlocks, oaks, maples and birches, the remnants of one of the mighty and famous forests of the globe. First of all in spring, the shadbush thrusts its beckoning sprays from a background of cross-hatched branches that take on a mauve or purple tone; then appear delicate leaves of green, yellow, rose, and all light shades of brown. Before crimson leaf buds top its branches in May, the blossoms of the American redbud cloud every twig with a rosy lavender for which there is no exact name, and the spicebush decks its aromatic twigs with

Photo: R. B. McFarland

Wooded shores of the West Branch near McGees Mills.

Photo: R. B. McFarland
Approaching Mahaffey, the West Branch flows through open meadows.

yellow flowerets. Mountain laurel blushes pink and rose; from its rich foliage, ever dark and glossy, rhododendron puts out white and pink bloom.

After its leaves have fallen, witch-hazel envelops itself in a cloud of pale yellow. The author cannot speak with authority for every mile of the river but she has been in few places where the lovely shrubs do not grow. It is perhaps not wholly to be regretted that innumerable motorists speed past the globes of delicate bloom without even asking what they are.

No doubt the Indians on the West Branch had foreseen their doom before the whites arrived. In their final struggle to hold their territory there was no general massacre like that in the Wyoming Valley, though many attacks were made on individuals or small groups that paddled canoes or pushed dugouts with iron-shod poles up the swift and shallow streams. One of the best-known tragedies had its first act in Union County, many miles from its consummation. Peter Grove and his brother started in pursuit of the assassins of their father. After nightfall they, and friends who accompanied them, came upon the war party asleep near the

Tree-lined banks of the West Branch with wooded hills in the distance as Curwensville is approached on Penna. 969.

Photo: R. B. McFarland

THE WEST BRANCH

mouth of a little stream now called Grove Run, which flows into Sinnemahoning Creek, and there killed all but one.

Nearby, decades after Indians had vanished from the neighborhood, seventeen skeletons of enormous size were discovered—evidence of a different sort of tragedy. They lay in a circle, their feet toward the ashes of a fire. It is supposed that these men were killed by lightning and that the clay roof of their hut eventually fell upon them. Hundreds of other bodies of which only the bones remain must lie beneath the forest soil along the banks of streams that were Indian highways.

As the quarrel between Great Britain and her American colonies became acute, the Indians were incited and supported by the Tories. Scalping the lonely hunter, dashing the brains of infants against the nearest tree, they undertook to clear the valley. Some of the pioneers had marched with the rifle company enlisting at Sunbury to report to General Washington at Cambridge; with them away, resistance was of necessity feeble.

Before the massacre in the Wyoming Valley, West Branch settlers were warned

Photo: J. Horace McFarland Co.
Underfoot in a West Branch forest—a carpet of ferns.

57

At Clearfield, on US 322, the West Branch lends its limpid beauty to a riverside park and playground.

Photo: R. B. McFarland

THE WEST BRANCH

by a friendly Indian; and later, whenever there was danger, Robert Covenhoven, a fearless scout, traveled swiftly along the tall ridges, avoiding the Indians and descending into the valleys to warn the settlers of danger. Abandoning their cabins, their gardens and little corn patches, they fled toward the forts and stockaded houses. Loading their belongings on boats if there was time, driving along the creek banks what livestock they could assemble, they looked back—to see perchance a red glow against the sky!

In the exodus called the Big Runaway in the fall of 1778 four-fifths of the West Branch population left their homes. As rapidly as possible they returned, to find their cabins still smoldering. Promptly two hundred troops under Colonel Thomas Hartley engaged the Indians in battle, destroyed the town of Queen Esther Montour and returned with cattle and other plunder. The settlers suffered a major loss in the death of Captain John Brady of a courageous family, who was shot from ambush. In 1779 there was another alarm as the Indians prepared to meet General Sullivan marching north to destroy their villages and crops. Again the settlers fled—now in the Little Runaway. Again some of those who remained behind were murdered; again flames reddened the shallow water.

Among those who visited the West Branch was, it is supposed, Etienne Brulé. It was through these valleys that Conrad Weiser was guided by his friend Shikellamy to the distant headquarters of the Six Nations at Onondaga. Count von Zinzendorf, the Moravian, and his followers glowingly described the country they visited. Various members of the Montour family, who were in the main friendly to the whites, had homes on the river.

The pioneer brought with him the powerful and accurate Pennsylvania German rifle, first made in Austria and developed and improved in Lancaster, York, Reading and Bethlehem. Game abounded; a few bison roamed the valleys, panthers and wolves lurked about and elk, deer, black bear and raccoons were common. Rabbits and squirrels made succulent stews; wild turkeys, quail and various waterfowl added variety to the menu. Had the settler found no animals, he could have survived on fish—pike, eel, trout, salmon and shad. Overhead in spring and fall, millions of passenger pigeons darkened the sky and when they roosted broke the large branches by the weight of their bodies. To destroy them required no powder but merely a net tossed over them as they slept.

PENNSYLVANIA'S SUSQUEHANNA

Today's traveler along the West Branch may decline to believe that for years it carried products of enormous value on its bosom. So shallow is it in periods of drought, so almost right-angled are some of its turns, so deep its valleys and sudden its descents that it is hard to imagine upon it even so light a vessel as a canoe. Yet at the present Cherry Tree in the southwest corner of Clearfield County began journeys that might end in Chesapeake Bay. In a spring freshet, on the other hand, it is not difficult to picture a sea-going yacht on certain expanded reaches. One may then be persuaded that around these curves, over or around these small cascades journeyed long vessels.

While the North Branch makes its quiet way over and beside beds of anthracite coal, unique and enormous reservoir of heat, light and power, the western sources of the West Branch, like the neighboring tributaries of the Allegheny, flow above beds of bituminous coal, far more widely scattered but less valuable per ton. Trans-

Photo: R. B. McFarland

Penna. 879 parallels the West Branch on the way to Shawville.

60

Photo: R. B. McFarland
In the plateau country the West Branch winds toward Surveyor.

ported as early as 1810 in high-sided flatboats called arks, which held from a thousand to twenty-five hundred bushels, it was sold in far-away settlements.

About 1840 the river began to transport its most valuable freight, more important than coal to the comfort and convenience of mankind. Coal is a source of light, heat and power. Wood is all this and is, in addition, material for buildings and the furnishing of buildings, for bridges and ships and piers, for railroad cars and the ties upon which they run. Without wood there would have been no civilization; to find substitutes for ever-dwindling supplies is the constant aim of science. For centuries man survived in cold climates without suspecting the deposits of coal in the earth. For centuries in the future he may still survive when coal is exhausted, provided he does not destroy the soil along with the timber.

The rivulets of the West Branch, flowing east from Cambria and Indiana counties, are joined at McGees Mills by Chest Creek and after another twenty-five miles, at Clearfield, once called Chinklacamoose, by Clearfield Creek. Rising in adjacent springs, the two are soon swung far apart by mountain ridges.

PENNSYLVANIA'S SUSQUEHANNA

The Moshannon, flowing from the south, adds a trace of darker blue to the line on the map but is itself colored yellow by clay. On nearby Mosquito Creek, in a wilderness of forest, steep hillside and rushing stream, Peter Karthaus erected a furnace to smelt surface iron. Remote from markets, he was successful for only a short time. East of the town that bears his name the river is best visited on foot or observed from an airplane. Good roads skirt the area but none attempts to accompany the river as it enters its fifty-mile course northeast and east through Clinton County, mountainous and spectacular in its scenery and somewhat humorous in its origin.

To this neighborhood, after many adventures, came a "New York Yankee" named Jerry Church. His school days had ended early, and he then earned his living in Canada, Pennsylvania, West Virginia, Kentucky, Illinois and Missouri and returned eventually to the East. Fortunately he recorded his almost incredible

Afternoon shadows on the hills at Karthaus.

Photo: R. B. McFarland

South of Keating, along US 120, the hills are wooded from peak to river.

adventures in a little volume that reads as though while writing he ran from one place to another.

Buying land adjoining Williamsport and Lewisburg on the West Branch, he divided it into lots and sold it at considerable profit. He then purchased a tract between the Susquehanna River and Bald Eagle Creek, divided it also and called it Lock Haven because of the locks in the canal and a raft haven in the river. Believing that Lycoming and Centre counties had more territory than they needed, he planned a new county to be called Eagle. His surgical operations were strongly objected to, but he succeeded in achieving his purpose when he appeared for the third time before the Legislature at Harrisburg. Eagle County they had rejected and were prepared to reject again, but they promptly accepted a county named Clinton, which they did not associate with Eagle. Lock Haven was made the county seat, and there Jerry sold more and more lots, built himself a house in a tree and completed his little book. Surely, no city or town had a more interesting "manager." Perhaps Jerry was the original member of that profession.

Photo: R. B. McFarland

Where US 120 crosses the West Branch near Hyner, there opens a lovely vista of river and hills forest-covered to their summits.

THE WEST BRANCH

"A Williamsport gentleman promised to be our partner and pay for one third, and we closed the bargain. At once I plotted out a town on paper and called it Lock Haven, for the two locks in the canal and the haven or harbor for the rafts on the river. We made public sale and sold a number of lots.

"I managed the town myself. All my sleeping partners left me; if there was music to be played I had to be a full band, having no person to assist. In order to carry out my originality, I built an office, standing eight feet above the ground. It was made by placing thirteen large pine trees, to represent our thirteen continental States, five feet in the ground, taking the bark off, and painting them in imitation of marble, with a fourteen-foot room inside of the posts. It was an odd-looking office, and different from any I had seen in this country.

"I built a summer-seat in a cluster of black walnut trees. It was twenty-five feet from the ground, forty feet long, and seven feet wide, bannistered, and a seat running all the way round, and winding stairs up one of the trees. I told a German painter to paint it like marble; but as he did not understand English very well, he made it what I call Dutch marble, all full of black and white spots. The natives thought it wonderful that I should so throw away my money to make a nice seat to sit on. It has ever since been called 'Church's Folly'."

By this time the lumber business of the West Branch had begun. One reason for the settlement of her North American colonies was the imperative need of Great Britain for ships. The forests of northern Europe were vanishing, and with a prospective shortage of timber went hope of conquest and colonization. There was, however, no reason for anxiety; extending inland in North America swept measureless forests. Even today in New England there remain pine trees marked to be used as masts for the King.

Watson's "Annals of Philadelphia" gives an account of one now forgotten and almost incredible pre-Revolutionary method of transporting to England timber felled nearer the coast than the Susquehanna. Hundreds of enormous logs were bound together, rigged with sails and navigated by experts. Eight hundred logs would make six ships of two hundred and fifty tons each. "An eye-witness who saw one of these mammoth fabrics descend into her destined element, said she bent and twisted much in launching, but when on the water looked to the eye of the beholder much like another ship in form."

PENNSYLVANIA'S SUSQUEHANNA

As farms and hamlets replaced the wilderness of trees near the coast, the vast wooded area of Pennsylvania was opened, not now to benefit the King of England, but to promote the progress of his rebellious colonies. The pioneer, paddling or poling his little craft up the West Branch, craning his neck to look with awe and wonder at the almost opaque ceiling, regarded the pines and hemlocks at first not as the source of enormous wealth but as almost sentient enemies. The crowns of the trees formed a nearly solid roof; the ground beneath was forever shadowed. Each tree limited the space of earth that could be cultivated; each trunk became an ambush for a murderous Indian.

The forest was rarely quiet. Water plunged over rocky ridges, sucked through trailing grasses. Some sounds were those that might be made by a dying man. The unending canopy murmured and whispered. Crows cawed mournfully, eagles uttered occasionally a thin feline wail, whip-poor-wills cried eerily, wolves howled and foxes barked. Always one listened for the war shout of an Indian. It was not strange that, each helping his neighbor, the pioneers swiftly girdled and burned the mammoth trees so that sunlight might sweeten the earth and make life safer. A pioneer felled a tree for his cabin, his furniture and his boat; soon a neighbor staked out his claim, and presently a dozen axes answered one another and the giant trees were laid side by side on the ground.

Most valuable of all the trees of Pennsylvania, strong as iron, abundant in growth, white pines lifted green heads in a belt seventy-five miles wide, stretching northeast from Bedford County. What was called the "quality stand" grew on the West Branch. Joseph Dudley Tonkin in his admirable little book, "The Last Raft," speaks of a hundred thousand board feet from a single acre. In this same space might grow also twenty thousand board feet of hemlock and hardwood.

Straight, so tall that it could be trimmed into a spar ninety feet long, a pine tree spliced to two of its fellows composed a mast measuring a hundred and forty feet. Not alone its height but its strength and resilience fitted it to bear an immense weight of canvas to all the seas of the world. Inured from a seedling to alternating cold and heat, drought and moisture, it remained unwarped, no matter what the weather. The tall pines John Bartram, the botanist, saw, with a height that he would not estimate because no one would believe him, grew east of the Susquehanna, along one of its tributaries. Such trees by the million composed

Photos: R. B. McFarland

One of the most picturesque river routes is US 120 between Lock Haven and Renovo.
Almost every turn of the road brings a charming view of river and mountains.

Photo: Courtesy Penna. Dept. of Forests and Waters

Of the "quality stand" of White Pine (*Pinus Strobus*) once so abundant on the West Branch only scattered trees remain today.

THE WEST BRANCH

the great forest along the West Branch. Of them a few survive in Middleswarth State Park in Snyder County, possibly because the depth of the ravine in which they grow made cutting difficult.

Presently the settlers became aware of the incalculable riches they possessed. Cities were rising, ships were being launched, mines timbered, railroad tracks laid. Into the forests peered representatives of those who already owned large sums of money and wished to acquire more. But how transport this unwieldly wealth to mills and shipyards?

The answer wound its way across meadows, crept through valleys and gorges, swung abruptly around rocky walls. In winter the streams were ice-bound; in summer they were almost dry. In spring, however, brooks became creeks and shallow stretches broadened into lakes. Coal had been carried on rafts—why not bind the huge timbers together, float them downstream and sell them when the journey was over? True, some stretches could not possibly carry the long heavy mass, but dams could be contrived and the water released when it was needed. Thus had General Clinton transported his soldiers on the Susquehanna below Lake Otsego. No doubt some of the West Branch pioneers had been Clinton's soldiers.

Photo: J. Horace McFarland
In August, the Joe-Pye-Weed (*Eupatorium purpureum*) blooms along streams.

A graceful bridge brings US 220 to Lock Haven. A park borders the West Branch, and the Bald Eagle mountain range forms a backdrop for the site of the prosperous city.

Photo: R. B. McFarland

THE WEST BRANCH

Gangs of lumbermen lived together in shanties or cabins, with a cook providing food. Labor was merely begun when the trees crashed to the ground, so cleverly thrown that they fell side by side where the growth was thick. Limbs must be lopped and boles cut to the right length. If it did not measure as much as was expected or if there was some imperfection, the long trunk was left to rot. Felled and trimmed, it must be moved to the stream to await the spring freshets. For a short distance it might be snubbed from tree to tree; otherwise it was drawn by teams of oxen or draft horses, sometimes eight pairs to one mammoth log. If cut on elevated land, a slide of snow and ice was made ready to quicken its progress.

Lashed side by side, with guiding oars fifty or sixty feet long fixed at front and back, a cabin for warmth and protection set up midway, the logs slipped downstream, now slowly, now with fearful rapidity. The crew must be forever watchful for rocks above or beneath the water, for falls that might speed the journey with a perilous plunge or make necessary the excavation of a canal. Halting the long raft required strength and skill; moving faster than the water, it was, to use Mr. Tonkin's simile, "a mixture of a one man track-meet and tying a knot in the tail of a red-eyed Hereford bull."

The market for masts was far away. No clipper ships were constructed at the villages of Lock Haven or Williamsport, or in the growing towns of Sunbury or Harrisburg, though various river settlements dreamed of building sea-going craft. Some expected to be ports for ocean travel. Rowboats, canal boats and Durham boats were built at many river ports, but the great masts were not meant for small boats. The markets were in Chesapeake or Delaware bays. It is said that through a spyglass a dealer in West Branch timber watched ships entering Philadelphia harbor, noting each defect and sending his men to recommend repairs in his master's shipyards. From all the ports where ships were built echoed the cry, "More West Branch pine!" In sixty years timber was cut to the value of two hundred and fifty million dollars.

The destination of the tall spars was not only American ports—Philadelphia, Baltimore, New York and Boston; they were set on ships in the Clyde. Coming and going around the world through the Strait of Magellan and around the Cape of Good Hope, the heavy masts swayed in the tempests but did not break.

In mid-century a different use was made of the river. No longer were only the

Photo: J. Horace McFarland

Great Hemlocks (*Tsuga canadensis*), State tree of Pennsylvania, were once worth more for tanbark than for lumber. They grew to enormous size in West Branch forests.

tall pines selected; now all timber was marketed, to be used for other purposes besides the masts of ships. Hemlock, which had been discarded because it would not hold square-cut nails, became usable with the invention of wire nails. Birch, beech, maple—all were cut. Short timbers were thrown into the river, creating new elements of danger. When they were halted by an obstruction or by a sharp curve, log drivers sought the key log that held back the jack-straw mass. No "tie-up" man struggling to hitch a raft to a tree found himself in such peril of death as the driver in a maelstrom of tossing logs. Sometimes rafts and logs formed a jam extending for six or seven miles.

Soon booms were constructed of logs chained together into which the floating timber was guided. Here, having been stamped as they were cut in the forest with the mark of their owner, the logs were sorted. At Lock Haven, Williamsport and other towns millions of feet of timber were assembled. Sometimes a chain broke and the escaping logs battered and perhaps destroyed the next boom down the river. Then all together floated toward Chesapeake Bay.

Mills were soon manufacturing the timber into materials for houses—doors, door frames, window frames, floor boards. Into the forest moved portable mills, and the shriek of their saws through hardwood was added to the ring of the axe. Large crews of men worked where there had been only a few. The forest presently furnished the railroad ties that promoted the assault on its very heart. Like harvested grain the trees fell. No gleaning was gathered. What was not carried away was left to rot or to furnish fuel for fires started by sparks from the engines.

A lover of the Susquehanna has begged that not too much be made of its floods, but no one can ask for the sake of the future that the horror of fire be underestimated or forgotten. The mirror of its water reflects the pure white of bloodroot and elder, the rose of laurel, the lavender and purple of asters, green of a thousand shades; it has also reflected—alas how often!—the orange light of fire, sometimes accidental, sometimes incendiary.

Both by word and by deed the raftsmen fiercely opposed the new and wholesale clearing of the forest by loggers. Some saw their lives threatened by plunging timber felled by the inexperienced; some protested in the name of conservation. The cutting of large trees had been selective; wholesale cutting meant utter destruction. Meetings of protest were held, courts were applied to, there was some

Photos: R. B. McFarland

From Antes Fort, Penna. 64 crosses the placid West Branch and a large island, then a second bridge to Jersey Shore.

THE WEST BRANCH

bloodshed. In deadly revenge long spikes were pounded into tree trunks so that the heads were hidden, and the saws driven by water power or steam burst as though exploded by dynamite.

The quarrel did not last forever; the years consumed in the destruction of the boundless forest were few. Commercial rafting began about 1835 and the last spars were floated in 1865. No longer did the rafts slide over waterfalls, rise like leaping horses above submerged rocks, or curve like a stone from a sling around the bases of cliffs. No longer did wives, mothers and sweethearts watch anxiously for the return of their men; no longer did Northumberland and Sunbury, Selinsgrove, Liverpool, Duncannon and Harrisburg, Marietta and Columbia hearken for the songs of the boatmen.

A few more decades and logs were neither rafted nor thrown into the river. Floods, especially in 1889, carried away the great booms, and transportation henceforth was by the railroads with numerous branches that penetrated the northern counties.

The flood of 1889 was a dreadful reality that cannot be omitted from any account of the Susquehanna, especially of its western tributaries, though the concentrated destruction and large loss of life at Johnstown have overshadowed the property loss at Williamsport and Sunbury. At South Fork on the Conemaugh the grim outline of the dam that added its waters to the flood already ten feet deep in the valley, is still visible. Along the Susquehanna there is no such memorial of ruin.

The storm that caused the chief disaster of Pennsylvania's history originated in the Rocky Mountains and moved eastward at a deliberate pace as though to draw into its thick clouds every drop of available moisture. Met above the ridge of the Allegheny Mountains by a wind from the east, it discharged in the neighborhood of four and a half billion tons of water in less than thirty-six hours. The West Branch and the Juniata had never failed to produce a ruinous flood at three inches of rain. Now the fall was eight inches.

The Johnstown flood has been vividly described by many of those who survived. One of the most interesting accounts of conditions on the Susquehanna, as well as on other rivers, is that by John Bach McMaster, the historian.

"Along the West Branch lie, in the order named, between the source and its

Photo: Courtesy James V. Brown Memorial Library
Under the Tiadaghton Elm, near Jersey Shore, a band of hardy pioneers declared their independence of George III, July 4, 1776.

mouth, the counties of Clearfield, Clinton, Cameron, Lycoming, Union and Northumberland. In each of them the storm began late in the afternoon of Memorial Day, which fell on Thursday and increased steadily in violence till Saturday morning. By that time every little creek and stream was sweeping the wreckage of all the farms along its banks into the West Branch.

"That a flood was imminent was first apparent at daylight on the morning of Friday, May 31st, when the headwaters of the West Branch were observed to be running twelve feet deeper than usual. At the town of Clearfield, as early as five in the morning, the river was running through the streets. When dusk came there were but five dry spots in the whole place, and these were covered long before midnight. At Renovo the river was brimful at five in the afternoon and one hour later the water entered the yards of those who lived on the river bank in the lower part of the town. By midnight three-quarters of the town was under water, the bridge carried away, the outhouses and sheds destroyed, the hotel ruined and the opera

76

THE WEST BRANCH

house demolished by a building carried down by the flood, the bottom washed out of the borough reservoir and hundreds of people driven from their homes. In some cases the very ground on which the houses stood was undermined and carried off. For miles down the river the banks were strewn with the wreckage, chairs from the opera house, furniture from the shops and dwellings, gates, outhouses and pieces of barns.

"At Lock Haven the damage was greater yet. The town stands in a deep valley at the junction of Bald Eagle creek with the West Branch and is concerned in the lumber trade. Early in the day messages had come by telephone from Clearfield announcing the flood at that place, and preparations had been made for high water. No one supposed that the flood could possibly reach the high-water mark of 1865. When, therefore, at eight o'clock in the evening the river began to rise no alarm was felt, though even then the rain was falling in torrents.

Photo: Courtesy James V. Brown Memorial Library
When lumber was king, the Williamsport boom held millions of board feet of logs.

77

No longer a lumber city, Williamsport, chief city of the West Branch, has many diversified manufactures, is a banking center and the county seat of Lycoming County.

Photo: G. Walter Colley

THE WEST BRANCH

"When toward midnight, the West Branch ran bank full, and a few minutes later water began pouring into the cellars of the houses the people for the first time realized that no common flood was upon them. Some left their homes and hurried to the houses of others on higher ground only to be again driven out. Some fled with valuable horses and cows to the hills or dragged them to the second stories. Hundreds sought refuge in the school house and the court house. At two in the morning the great lumber boom gave way and millions of feet of logs went down the river on their way to Chesapeake Bay. Before dawn the water of the West Branch and Bald Eagle creek had joined and turned the valley from hill to hill into a vast lake of rushing water. Sidewalls were torn up. Stables and outbuildings, barns and coal-sheds and wood-houses were swept away. Sawlogs and driftwood, boards and piles, littered the streets as the flood went whirling through the town. The gas works and electric light plant were destroyed and the town left in darkness.

"At four in the afternoon on Saturday, June 1st, when the flood stopped rising, the city was completely submerged and the water three feet deeper than in 1865. From every part of Clinton county now came a report of farms damaged, of crops washed away, of bridges broken down, of roadsides cut, of mills destroyed, of trains wrecked, of lives lost.

"Rushing down the river the flood reached Williamsport in the early hours of the morning of June 1st, and before noon the history of Lock Haven was repeated. At two in the morning the water in the West Branch was seventeen feet deep, and rising rapidly. At three the 75,000,000 feet of lumber from Lock Haven, set free by the breaking of the Lock Haven boom, began to run into the boom of Williamsport. The logs it was thought could be held on a twenty-foot flood—but when, at three thirty, the water was running nineteen feet deep, and the rain still falling in sheets, it became apparent to all that the boom must go. At nine it went out and 150,000,000 feet of sawlogs began a journey to Chesapeake Bay. Then followed every kind of manufactured lumber, sashes and door frames, pickets and shingles, from the yards along the river bank, mills, bridges, houses and trees. The railroad station was swept of everything movable. The track was washed out and littered with broken cars, boards, trees and sand; and communication of every sort was destroyed. Three-fourths of the city was under water and more than one-half of the people were sufferers from the flood.

Approaching Williamsport from the south on US 15, there is a breath-taking view from Bald Eagle Mountain overlooking Montoursville and the confluence of Loyalsock Creek.

Photo: R. B. McFarland

THE WEST BRANCH

"Below Williamsport, lumber, logs, broken buildings lined the shores, or lay stranded in heaps on the islands. At Montgomery four spans and from five to eight feet of the stone piers of the Philadelphia and Erie Railroad bridge were carried off. Then went the Dewart bridge. Floating down the river these two soon came in contact with the river-road bridge at Milton, lifted it from its piers and together dashed into the Reading Railroad bridge, tore out a span, and, a few moments later, wrecked the Lewisburg and Northumberland Railroad bridge. Meanwhile the water had overflowed the flats above the town, had crossed Upper Milton, and, entering Milton, met the back-water of Limestone creek and covered the South Ward of the city. At Summit almost the entire town was covered, and the valley up and down as far as the eye could reach was one great lake. It was three in the morning of Sunday before the flood began to go down. Milton was by this time a ruined city—bridges, churches, factories, private homes, stores, streets, pavements, cisterns, wells, all were damaged."

The Johnstown flood is remembered by few. To the living men who had a part in the rafting it also seems like a dream. If any young reader hears his senior say, "I can still see the long rafts come downstream," let him plead for more. In 1938 a company of experienced men undertaking to live again the glories of their youth, started at McGees Landing and succeeded in piloting their carefully constructed raft as far as Muncy. There, under the eyes of hundreds of observers, it swung against a bridge pier and when it righted itself some of its passengers were struggling in the swift water. Of these seven were drowned. The raft itself was piloted as far as Harrisburg and there, as in the old days, the timber was sold.

Not only had unscientific and wasteful cutting destroyed the forests with their protection against flood, but thousands of acres of soil had been robbed of life. The succeeding growth was sparse, the timber of low grade. When the precious humus from the wood rotting on the ground was washed away, rivulets, once confined in channels, coursed in sheets down steep hillsides, carrying wealth from the land to the ocean, which has no use for humus.

Fortunately, Pennsylvania awakened to the waste and destruction of her possessions before it was too late, and on many of her hillsides along the West Branch forests have been planted, already beautiful and valuable, though never to equal the giants growing into majesty over two or three centuries.

Eagles Mere, peerless Pennsylvania lake in the Susquehanna area, is reached easily by US 220 and Penna. 42 east of Montoursville or from the charming town of Muncy by Penna. 405, US 220 and Penna. 42.

Photo: Victor Dallin

THE WEST BRANCH

One of the few diversions of the rafters and the loggers was singing. For the collection and classification of the songs that are remembered we are indebted to Colonel Henry W. Shoemaker. Round the campfire, in the shanties, on rafts, the lumbermen sang, their accompaniment a violin, mouth organ, accordion or sometimes an ancient dulcimer or harp. Hither the English brought their ballads "Barbara Allen" and "Kitty Maury." Loggers from Canada added their French songs, and the Irish sang of Finnegan's wake.

Some airs were lively; perhaps more were sad. There was no mocking-bird in the north woods, but how he chanted over Hallie's grave and how Lorena and Nellie Gray were mourned! Methodist hymns were popular; Civil War songs were sung over and over. When the boys of Driftwood tucked bucks' tails into their military caps and shouldered their muskets in 1861, their friends sang,

> "They left their mountain home,
>   Where oft they chased the deer;
> They left their families all alone,
>   Without a sigh or fear."

His fellows taunted one who did not go,

> "You with the terrible warlike mustaches,
>   Fit for a colonel or chief of a clan,
> You with a waist made for sword-belt and sashes,
>   Where are your shoulder-straps, sweet little man?"

Importing a song from Maine, woodsmen gloried in their strenuous life.

> "The music of our burnished axe shall make the woods resound,
>   And many a lofty, ancient pine shall tumble to the ground;
> At night, ho! round our good campfire we'll sing while rude winds blow
> O, we'll range the wild woods over, while a lumbering we'll go."

Who could fail to join in the plea to the girls of Lushbaugh, a settlement along the Sinnemahoning? How could the Lushbaugh girls refuse to accept the invitation?

> "Oh, Lushbaugh girls, are you coming out tonight,
>   Coming out tonight, coming out tonight?
> Oh, Lushbaugh girls, are you coming out tonight—
>   To dance by the light of the moon?"

PENNSYLVANIA'S SUSQUEHANNA

Few writers about this area have been able to resist the following rhymed comment on a boom town:

> "There is a place called Sinnamahone
> Of which but little good is known;
> For sinning, ill must be its fame,
> Since Sin begins its very name.
> So well indeed its fame is known
> That people think they should begin
> To drop the useless word Mahone,
> And call the country simply Sin!"

At Keating, having been swelled by the romantic waters of the Sinnemahoning and its tributaries, the river turns north and northeast. Kettle Creek, entering at Westport, descends from distant springs adjacent to those that feed the St. Lawrence. From it rises not only the music of the stream but the ethereal echoes of a great violin played by a master. A hundred years ago Ole Bull, famous Norwegian violinist, gave a concert at Williamsport, the population of which then numbered two thousand. The union of Norway and Sweden had been felt by the Norwegians as cruelly oppressive, and Bull had pleaded in vain for his people's political freedom. Upon it, he was confident, depended their development and that of a national drama and music. In Pennsylvania he believed he might establish a colony where freedom would flourish.

No doubt he spoke of his project when he visited Williamsport, and he was thereupon escorted by a speculator to the deep valley of Kettle Creek. Here was no ocean, here were no tide-filled fiords, but there were majestic trees and deep valleys, clear health-giving air and a pure stream. The soil was fertile—one could tell that by the trees. By this time a railroad followed the Susquehanna, and a railroad and a canal crossed New York not far away. Certain that he could establish his people in prosperity, he purchased a hundred and twenty thousand acres in Potter County and secured an option on almost an equal area in McKean County.

The colonists numbered eventually three or four hundred. At a formal opening, when citizens from neighboring sections welcomed the strangers, Bull improvised a musical composition and reminded his people of the peace and plenty of the new land. On the steep side of a hill overlooking Kettle Creek he built himself a

Photo: R. B. McFarland

Along the West Branch north of Montgomery, rise the curiously peaked Muncy Hills, and beyond them the town of Muncy.

Photo: R. B. McFarland

A turn from Penna. 405 in Watsontown, famed for manufacture of bricks, brings one to a river park and the graceful bridge crossing the West Branch to White Deer.

house that he called Walhalla, and the spring below he named for the island of Lyso in Norway. The settlements were Norway, New Bergen and Oleona.

Either he had been willfully deceived, or he had been careless in his purchase of the land and neglected to have the title investigated. He had no claim upon what he had paid for, and his people owned nothing; in despair many departed, some to join Norwegians in Wisconsin and Minnesota.

The names of the settlements remain. The hills that Bull loved are shorn of their great pines and either farmed or covered with second growth. Above the site of the log castle float the flag of the United States and the flag—not of Sweden and Norway that Bull despised—but of Norway alone.

At North Bend, once called Young Woman's Town because of the slaying of a captive, the river swings sharply southeast into a rugged and lonely region. Many of the hills are again wooded, their timber extremely valuable if fire does not destroy it. The mountain pageant from Hyner's View is so vast that railroads, bridges and houses shrink into the background and the landscape with its winding river appears as it was when the woodsman first lifted his axe upon the living trees, or the long rafts slipped round the curves.

At Jerry Church's Lock Haven enters from the south Bald Eagle Creek, the first northward-flowing tributary east of the Moshannon. Here empty two drainage systems with the inevitable result when thaws soften the ice and at the same time spring rains pour.

From almost the northern border of the State flows Pine Creek, notable for various reasons. The first is the gorge on its upper course, now part of Harrison State Park. The rim is accessible by a paved highway, and from there one may look down a thousand feet and understand why the Indians called the stream Tiadaghton or Lost Creek. It is difficult to believe that thousands of enormous trees bound into rafts were floated around its abrupt turns, but easy to visualize the slides of snow and ice on which they coasted to the river.

On the upper sources of Pine Creek one's spirit is uplifted by the beauty of sky and forest; where it joins the West Branch one is uplifted for another reason. Here on the 4th of July, 1776, unaware of a similar gathering in Philadelphia, a company with rifles in hand met under an elm to declare themselves free of Great Britain. The elm still stands, twenty-one feet in circumference, a reminder of the

Opposite the thriving town of Milton, a turn from US 15 at Central Oak Heights enables the traveler to overlook the site of Shikellamy Town, once an Indian settlement in the widening valley.

Photo: R. B. McFarland

THE WEST BRANCH

spirit of our fathers. Some of those who met here were "Fair Play" men who had already set up their own tribunal in the wilderness.

The river approaches Williamsport in wide curves. Through the center of the busy city and a few miles to the east flow Lycoming and Loyalsock creeks. Both rise in wild and romantic country. A few minutes in a car and the traveler may watch for trout in unsullied waters; a little longer and he may look down from the heights of Bald Eagle Ridge.

Muncy Creek flows from headwaters in Sullivan County, another area of beauty where Eagles Mere lies high in the hills. Of this section an illustrated account has been published in "Eagles Mere and the Sullivan Highlands" by Dr. J. Horace McFarland and Robert B. McFarland, long summer residents.

In their introduction they say: "In a roughly rectangular stretch of territory between the two great river branches which unite at Sunbury to form the broad-flowing Susquehanna, lies the small, gem-like Lake of the Eagles, not in one of the wooded valleys but actually on top of a mountain. The Sullivan Highlands, which give Eagles Mere its forest setting, stretch northeastward to the North Branch of the Susquehanna where that stream makes the eastward swing of a great elbow; southeastward the great mass of North Mountain marks the limit of the Highlands, with lesser hills and cultivated fields reaching to the Susquehanna's North Branch where it flows westward. Southwestwardly the transition from highland to lowland is more gradual, giving from the mountain tops, broad vistas of forest-covered lesser hills and the cultivated lands bordering on the West Branch of the Susquehanna toward Williamsport; to the northwest the limit of the Sullivan Highlands can be defined by Lycoming and Towanda Creeks.

"Originally covered by the magnificent forest characteristic of Penn's Woods, this region was rather ruthlessly despoiled by the wasteful lumbering of the latter part of the nineteenth century, first for its pines, later for the tan-bark of its hemlocks, and still later for its hardwoods. After the lumbering came the scourge of fire, so that today there are but few places where one may see stands of the primeval forest that was the glory of Pennsylvania. Forest protection under the wise supervision of the Pennsylvania Department of Forests and Waters and interested private ownership, has resulted in a return to good forest conditions, not matching the half-millenium original growth, but providing valuable 'crops' of forest prod-

US 15 skirts Lewisburg, site of Bucknell University. Turn on Penna. 45 through the town to reach the West Branch, where from South Water Street the river is seen with Montour Mountain beyond.

Photo: R. B. McFarland

THE WEST BRANCH

ucts, and providing a region rich in recreational facilities within overnight reach of twenty million people of the eastern United States."

Now the river turns south, as if going about its business at last. Its curves are gentle; it flows placidly through broader valleys and past pleasant towns. Lovely White Deer Creek enters at Allenwood, and Buffalo Creek at Lewisburg. The view of Bucknell University from across the river should be, perhaps has been, a lure to students.

At last round Blue Hill, and the West Branch is no more. On the perpendicular face of the cliff imagination has long since traced a stern profile and named it appropriately for Shikellamy the Oneida, sent by the Six Nations to watch over the lands claimed by his people. Here passed the long rafts, here flood-borne timber sped downstream, here from bank to bank puffed little steamers, here canal boats crept round the tall cliff. From here, looking over the brink, one may see today the logs that formed the foundation of the ancient West Branch covered bridge, predecessor of the present concrete bridge. From here is visible a new meeting of the waters.

Photo: J. Horace McFarland Co.
In July, the Elder (*Sambucus canadensis*) displays masses of white bloom.

Photo: Courtesy The Pennsylvania Railroad
Among the rushes of the upper Juniata near Aliquippa Gap hide the waterfowl.

THE JUNIATA

"Magnificent morning river fog in a hill country—lying smoothly level till slant sun warms the crests, then quivering, undulating, bursting out mushroom forms and sending flocks of sheepy offspring floating up the side valleys to dissipate in delicate iridescence on the higher slopes. For twenty miles the scene unfolded glacier white and still at first, as if death lay under. Only the farmer, early laborer, tramp, and sleepless watcher by sick bed see this show and treasure it, never satiated. A warming thought, that the common people garner most of earth's beauty; artist and æsthete but tiny fractions.

"There life was prolonged by going from night into clear day on the ridge, then down to valley fog gloam, emerging hours later easting into a second morn with a roomy day ahead."

—FREDERIC BRUSH
"Walk the Long Years," 1946

A FEW MILES NORTH of Duncannon, the Juniata adds its volume to the main river. Having cut at right angles through the lower ridges of the Alleghenies, it flows east, then northeast, in curves that follow the wider curves of the West Branch. It is described somewhat inaccurately in the stanza known to all.

"Wild roved an Indian girl,
Bright Alfarata,
Where sweep the waters
Of the blue Juniata."

Except in times of excessive rainfall the flow of the waters is placid and their color oftener brown than blue. Also, the poem bestows an unlikely name upon its heroine, "Alfarata," perhaps to rhyme with Juniata, a corruption of the Indian Onojutta.

The most remote Juniata springs rise in Somerset County, well to the west of the center of the State. Gathering in tiny Raystown Creek, they enter Bedford County through a gap in the mountain wall and flow northeast toward Bedford Town, where historians and story writers continue to find rich material. Here, two hundred years ago, was situated a British military post, alert to the menace of Indians and French. When the Indians had withdrawn from other areas, the report would still be made: "All quiet except at Bedford!"

Photo: R. B. McFarland
Near Hopewell, Penna. 26 runs close to the Raystown Branch.

In the first volume of his "Winning of the West" Theodore Roosevelt describes in a few vivid words the isolation of the American pioneer. The destruction of the forest was caused not always by the need for wood for cabins and furniture but by the terror of midnight at noon.

"Up to the door-sills of the log huts stretched the solemn and mysterious forest. There were no openings to break its continuity; nothing but endless leagues of shadowy wolf-haunted woodland. The great trees towered aloft till their separate heads were lost in the mass of foliage above, and the rank underbrush choked the spaces between the trunks. On the higher peaks and ridge crests of the mountains there were straggling birches and pines, hemlocks and balsam firs; elsewhere oaks, chestnuts, hickories, maples, beeches, walnuts, and great tulip trees. The sunlight could not penetrate the roofed archway of murmuring leaves; through the gray aisles of the forest men walked always in a kind of mid-day gloaming. Those who lived in the open plains felt when they came to the back-woods as if their heads were hooded.

THE JUNIATA

"All the land was shrouded in one vast forest. It covered the mountains from crest to river-bed, filled the plains, and stretched in sombre and melancholy wastes toward the Mississippi. All that it contained, all that lay within it and beyond it, none could tell; men only knew that their boldest hunters, however deeply they had penetrated, had not yet gone through it."

Through the dark forest, in and along the little Juniata tributaries men, women and children fled from Indians, their last breath expended in cries of agony. The most harrowing history is that of the Tull family on Tull's hill on the Juniata watershed, a short distance west of Bedford. Father, mother and nine daughters were massacred; only the single son survived.

Across rocky fords armies dragged their cannon—Americans in hunting shirts, Highlanders in kilts, British in scarlet. At Bedford Town Benjamin Franklin rode south for his meeting with General Braddock; here President Washington turned

Photo: R. B. McFarland
The Raystown Branch of the Juniata winds through the hills near Saxton.

95

From Water Street on US 22, the Frankstown Branch of the Juniata marked the "Warrior Trail" for Indians traveling west and south.

Photo: R. B. McFarland

THE JUNIATA

back when he found the Whiskey Rebellion subsiding. Through rough streams splashed Anthony Wayne, planning to subdue the Western Indians; through them rode Aaron Burr, dreaming of empire for himself.

A Pennsylvanian, Conrad Richter, has recounted in "The Trees," a fine piece of Americana, the experience of a family tramping from Pennsylvania to Ohio after most of the Indians had gone. The landscape under the eager eyes of the heroine, young Sayward, was duplicated whenever pioneers climbed the ridges of the Susquehanna watershed.

"For a moment Sayward reckoned that her father had fetched them unbeknownst to the Western ocean and what lay beneath was the late sun glittering on green-black water. Then she saw that what they looked down on was a dark, illimitable expanse of wilderness. It was a sea of solid treetops broken only by some gash where deep beneath the foliage an unknown stream made its way. As far as the eye could reach, this lonely forest sea rolled on and on till its faint blue billows broke against an incredibly distant horizon.

"They had all stopped with a common notion and stood looking out. Sayward saw her mother's eye search with the hope of finding some settlement or leastwise a settler's clearing. But over that vasty solitude no wisp of smoke arose. Though they waited here till night, the girl knew that no light of human habitation would appear except the solitary red spark of some Delaware or Shawanee campfire. Already the lowering sun slanted melancholy rays over the scene, and as it sank, the shadows of those far hills reached out with long fingers."

Near Bedford the Raystown Creek is enlarged by tributaries from north and south. Dunning Creek, originating in springs in the Allegheny Mountains, flows quietly in ordinary times, but the elevation of its sources and the ruthless removal of forests justifies alarm when rains begin.

The streams from the south flow from springs impregnated with sulphur and lime, magnesia and chalybeate. Traveling on horseback, in gigs, coaches and stages, the rheumatic journeyed thither. Buildings erected to shelter those who sought health or tried to escape the heat of southern summers, spread through the valley and climbed the steep hillside. Great men came and went; beautiful ladies danced in the ballrooms. John C. Calhoun, Daniel Webster, Henry Clay, Thaddeus Stevens remained for brief periods or weeks of rest.

Where US 22 crosses the Juniata, east of Huntingdon, the river seems practically surrounded by mountains.

Photo: R. B. McFarland

THE JUNIATA

Toward the close of the Second World War, the historic hotel became a place of mystery. Motorists were warned away by guards; pedestrians were discouraged from approaching. No sound was heard from within, but short-statured men and women, said to be civilian representatives—ambassadors and ministers and their families—of a nation that had made war upon the United States, were visible in the grounds and on the long verandas. As quietly as they came they were taken away, to begin their long journey to the far eastern country that was their home. Surely, since the Indians were dispossessed, no stranger company drank the medicinal water of these Susquehanna springs in the deep cleft of the mountains!

Before canals were dug and railroads built, mammoth covered wagons toiled up the steep hills, drivers shouting, dogs barking. The downward journey was tuned to another sound, that of shrieking brakes. The powerful horses, sometimes as many as sixteen to a wagon, stood still in the little streams, the cool water bathing their pasterns. Westward moved the manufactured and imported goods of the East, eastward the corn and whiskey of the West. Eastward moved also droves of cattle, horses and pigs and flocks of turkeys and geese; they, too, refreshed themselves where rivulets crossed the road or where spring-filled troughs invited.

Today motorcars speed where once huge wagons lumbered. No approach to the Juniata is more beautiful than that of the Lincoln Highway westward from Chambersburg—now in a rich, cultivated valley, now between apple orchards, now on the heights of the Allegheny Plateau from which one may see ridge after ridge sweeping northeast from Maryland. The springs on their flanks contribute first to the Juniata, then to the West Branch.

One cannot err in selecting any season for this journey, but certainly none is lovelier than fall. The general tone of the landscape seen from on high is blue, with the valleys deepening to gray. Sassafras, dogwood, beech, maple are aflame in a thousand shades. The streams mirror sprays of aster—white, pink, lavender, purple. Thickets of hemlock and rhododendron form backgrounds for the enormous maroon leaves of young oaks. Sumac mingles its dark red with the gray feathers of fading goldenrod; the delicate yellow bloom of witch-hazel catches the eye of its lover. In the valleys the willows and locusts are soft gray, the trunks and branches of the mammoth sycamores cream-white.

Northeast in deep, thickly shaded, narrow valleys, flow the fern-edged sources

Penna. 76, a connecting road from US 22 near Mill Creek, crosses the Juniata River, then ascends the east side of Sideling Hill. Near the summit is a view of the Juniata where it passes through Jack's Narrows. The hillside scars are quarries for sand used for refractories, produced in this region.

Photo: R. B. McFarland

THE JUNIATA

of the Conodoguinet, which enters the Susquehanna opposite Harrisburg. Parnell Knob stands out against the vast dome of the sky; ahead is the mass of North Mountain and farther on rises the steep wall of Sideling Hill. Beyond Ray's Hill the little streams empty into Raystown Creek, which has grown larger as it flowed east, with many curves, past Will and Evitt mountains, and through a gap in Martin's Hill Mountain.

Ray's Hill allows no slipping round or through but peremptorily blocks the creek, called now the Raystown Branch of the Juniata. Henceforth its flow is northeast in a fertile limestone valley, between Ray's Hill and Sideling Hill on the east and Tussey Mountain on the west. Spiraling through Bedford County and thence into Huntingdon, it empties eventually into the Juniata at Ardenheim.

In the gap of Martin's Hill Mountain lies a pretty town, Everett, long called Bloody Run. The dreadful name kept in memory an assault upon a pack train carrying rum and guns to the Indians, a present from His Majesty King George. It was certain that, drunken with the rum and armed with the muskets, the Indians would massacre the whites. When the colonial government paid no heed to the pleas of the settlers, they took the law into their own hands.

Roughly paralleling the Raystown Branch on the west side of Tussey Mountain, the Frankstown Branch flows northeast. It is smaller than the Raystown Branch and equally placid until the ice thaws suddenly or spring rains pour. Before it empties into the Juniata it passes Hollidaysburg, once a town of great importance. Here ended the Susquehanna Canal, and here began the famous Portage road where boats divided into sections were carried to the summit of the Allegheny Mountain and let down to another canal fed by the Kiskiminitas.

Near the sources of Dunning Creek, other springs draining from the steep flank of Allegheny Mountain unite to form the Little Juniata, which, flowing north between Allegheny and Brush mountains, makes an abrupt turn east at Tyrone. Between two ridges of Brush Mountain lies Sinking Spring Valley, where from under a limestone arch gushes a famous spring. Its outlet, Lost and Found Creek, disappears and reappears, passes under Cave Mountain and emerges at Water Street, so called because in the narrow space left by the crowding mountains the wagon road coincided with the stream bed.

Having swung east at Tyrone, the Little Juniata bisects Huntingdon County.

PENNSYLVANIA'S SUSQUEHANNA

At the sharp curve enters the smaller of two Bald Eagle creeks; the other joins the West Branch at Lock Haven. Both creeks were called thus for Chief Bald Eagle, and it is not uncommon to see one of the great birds for which chief and mountain and streams were named.

Here, as on the southern headwaters of the Juniata, the Indians took heavy toll. Hollidaysburg was named for a massacred family. In the thick woods white men in terror of the law sought refuge. Here lived also, the inhabitants believed, warlocks and witches casting spells, telling the lovelorn how to find mates and the wicked how to gain revenge. Here roamed strange animals, some of whom could speak; an enormous white stag appeared for years as a black ghost of himself. To this day traditions of mighty hunters and trappers are treasured.

This was not the area of towering white pines or thick dark hemlocks, but there were other trees in abundance. In Sinking Spring Valley the Indians had

A graceful bend in the Juniata at Newton-Hamilton.

Photo: R. B. McFarland

Near McVeytown, as the Juniata flows east, there is more cultivated land.
Photo: R. B. McFarland

found lead for their bullets. Surface iron was either smelted by the white men in small furnaces or hauled to Pittsburgh. The product of chief importance was grain reaped in the fertile coves and floated as far as Baltimore, first on the river, then on the canal.

Fortunate is the student of the Susquehanna who discovers the voluminous material assembled by the Pennsylvania Railroad and generously shared. Information is not compiled by statisticians only; a large portion is recorded by the lover of nature. In no section is this more true than that traversed by the Juniata. William Sipes, writing seventy-five years ago, prepares the traveler for a journey from Tyrone to Duncannon. Much has been changed since he wrote so enthusiastically, but the essential loveliness remains.

"The miniature river in its course of a hundred miles through the mountains, has overcome the obstacles in its way by strategy as well as by power. At many places it has dashed boldly against the wall and torn it asunder; at others it winds tortuously round the obstruction — creeping stealthily through secret valleys and

Photos: R. B. McFarland

Penna. 103 from Lewistown to Mt. Union is longer and more picturesque than US 22. Here, near Granville and beyond Mattawana, the Pennsylvania Railroad follows the Juniata closely. Cultivated fields in the valley are backed by wooded mountains.

secluded glens. At some points the mountains appear to have retired from the attacking current leaving numerous isolated hills standing as sentinels to watch its progress.

"The severed mountains, the towering embankments and the sentinel hills are all joined into form and molded into shape by the action of the elements and the foliage of nature, leaving no abrupt precipices and few naked rocks to mar the uniform beauty. The valleys and many of the hills are brought under cultivation and some of the latter rise in the distance, presenting alternate squares of yellow, green and brown, while their summits are crowned with the clumps of forest trees, indicating the luxuriance of growth before the march of civilization invaded it.

"The morning mist often shrouds mountains and valleys. The tints of evening spread over them golden and purple halos while dense shadows creep up the wooded embankments. Spring clothes the entire landscape in tender green, summer deepens this into a darker tint and intersperses it with the yellow of ripening harvest. Autumn lights up the forests with the bright hues of changing foliage and winter spreads its pure mantle of white."

Spruce and Shaver creeks enter the river from the north and at Petersburg the Frankstown Branch flows in from the south. Tussey Mountain opens to leave a path for the creek and the Branch and the highway and the railroad. Upon the steep lower slopes the eye of the engineer fixes itself as the streams rise. The river— it is the Little Juniata no more—has allowed the highway and the railroad, and long ago the canal as well, to take advantage of its passes and from time to time, as if to show its power, it reclaims what it has given. Then names otherwise little known to the world—Frankstown Branch, Spruce Creek, Shaver Creek, Beechwood, Barree—appear on the front page. When the river rises, the tall hills are separated not by valleys but by lakes and seas. The record rise had been in 1847, until in 1889, it rose eight feet higher. Then, in Huntingdon County, not a bridge remained.

In March, 1936, a variety of conditions conspired to set the scene again for widespread destruction. Only twice before, in 1889 and 1894, had there been commensurate rainfalls and both had occurred in late May when the soft earth could immediately absorb a portion of the water. Now the earth was still frozen and masses of ice remained. In the upper regions of every stream torrents swept away

Flowing past Lewistown, county seat of Mifflin County, the Juniata describes a graceful S-curve, to disappear seemingly in the middle distance where it enters Lewistown Narrows. In the foreground is a plant of The Viscose Company, the world's largest producer of rayon. Kishacoquillas Creek, which here joins the Juniata, drains a beautiful and fertile valley.

Photo: Courtesy The Kepler Studio, Lewistown, Penna.

every obstruction. The forests that once stayed the course of floods down the sides of the mountains were gone. The lakes that formed in the lowlands were not placid but boiling, wave-broken expanses. Where earlier there had been villages there were now towns, from which the inhabitants must flee.

Surrounded by hills, bisected by the river, lies the town of Huntingdon, once called Standing Stone from an ancient monolith fourteen feet high engraved with picture writing. When the Indians were made to understand that their hills and valleys were theirs no longer, they carried the stone away. A replica in size occupies the site of the monument, and the Borough of Huntingdon pictures it on its seal.

The modern name has an interesting origin. Gratified by the generous response of Selina, Countess of Huntingdon, to his appeal for funds, Provost William Smith of the then new University of Pennsylvania, named in her honor the territory of which he was proprietor. The present inhabitants are mindful of her interest in education; up and down the steep and beautiful hills and into villages from Warriors Mark to Orbisonia, from McAlevys Fort to Roberts Lake, flies the bookmobile of the County library, called affectionately Selina. From no better vantage point than a seat beside the librarian may one observe the Juniata.

On the hill west of Huntingdon is Juniata College, of the Church of the Brethren, formerly called Dunkers, who like Moravians and Mennonites accepted the sanctuary offered by William Penn. When the farming areas of Lancaster County were pre-empted, many "plain people" moved up the fertile valleys of the Susquehanna. Wearing a simple garb but for the most part enlightened and valuing education, they have contributed to the nation not only tillers of the soil but clergymen, educators and men of many other professions. Two of the Juniata College buildings are modeled upon the buildings of Ephrata Cloister, situated upon Cocalico Creek, a smaller Susquehanna tributary in Lancaster County.

At Ardenheim, having wound and twisted its way from Everett, its course suggesting the shaft of a corkscrew, the Raystown Branch at last adds its substantial contribution to the river. To the east, the gates of the mountain open. At Mapleton the river pushes its way through Jack's Mountain by way of Jack's Narrows, into long narrow Mifflin County, tending like the mountains and the river, from southwest to northeast. At Mt. Union, said to have been named from

East of Lewistown are the Lewistown Narrows, a trough between mountains through which the Juniata winds gracefully. The Pennsylvania Railroad main line follows the south bank, US 22 and 322 the north bank.

Photo: Courtesy The Pennsylvania Railroad

the conjunction of many mountains, one may see long slides on the steep hillsides. Some appear gray, some white; some are smooth and hard, others are a torrent of loose rocks. On some a sharp eye can detect workmen and machinery near the summit. Crushed and combined with limestone, the stone is molded into refractory brick for the lining of furnaces or ground into sand for the finest of glass. The new lens at Palomar in California is a product of Mt. Union sand.

Though it is swelled by storied Aughwick Creek, the river cannot force its way through Blacklog Mountain. The original inhabitants doubtless pronounced Aughwick in guttural tones; it is now a snappy "Ow-ick." When the Indians complained with good reason that the settlers had come farther than the treaties allowed, the provincial government commanded them to leave. Disobeyed, the government used force and finally burned the cabins of the intruding whites, thus postponing bloodshed for a while but only for a while.

The river hugs the flank of Blacklog Mountain, swings across the valley against Jack's Mountain and back against Blue Mountain. At its conjunction with Kishacoquillas Creek is Lewistown, beautiful for situation and famed for its industries, once the home of Shawanee Indians who called it Ohesson.

Kishacoquillas Creek drains the southern portion of the Seven Mountains, a rugged, thickly forested area. The lower course of the creek is bordered on both sides by steel plants. In this valley lived John Logan, older son of Shikellamy, who was deprived of the leadership of his people by the loss of an eye. Compelled to leave the Susquehanna lands, he settled in southwestern Pennsylvania and when his family was massacred he moved into Ohio. The mournful lament recited by school-children and attributed to him comes with profound effect from the son of the great chief, once ruler of the vast Susquehanna area and friend of the white man.

The upper valley is occupied by the straitest sect of Amish Mennonites. Here, eschewing not only the vanities of the world but most of its conveniences, they live at peace. In his account of the Pennsylvania Germans, Dr. Russell W. Gilbert divides this small group into eight varieties according to masculine coiffeurs and costumes. "Nebraskas" let their hair grow till it touches the shoulders; "Peach-eyites" trim halfway up the ear. The most "plain" wear two suspenders of wool; the most nearly worldly, two of elastic; those between, one elastic and one wool.

Wooded mountains and cultivated fields from the Port Royal bridge.

The curious traveler who seeks to make their acquaintance may as well stay away unless he can speak Pennsylvania German. Especially should he stay away if he is disposed to laugh at what seems to the Amish right and proper.

From Lewistown the river curves south and then north, to slip through a succession of narrows between the southern tip of Shade Mountain and the northern tip of Blue Ridge. When the Pennsylvania Railroad began to lay its tracks along the river, there was no house for ten miles.

At Port Royal enters the Juniata's last large tributary from the south. This is Tuscarora Creek, flowing through Tuscarora Valley, the scene of a dramatic ride. When General Lee, venturing hopefully into Pennsylvania, turned east at Chambersburg to move toward Gettysburg, his whereabouts were unknown to President Lincoln and the Union Army, since all telegraphic communication was cut off. From Chambersburg, Harrisburg could be reached by way of Port Royal, where there were Union troops. Scout Stephen Pomeroy rode fifty-two miles, first dragging his horse up over Tuscarora Mountain, today pierced by one of the tunnels

THE JUNIATA

of the Pennsylvania Turnpike, then along Tuscarora Creek. His relatives in the valley furnished him with fresh horses and sped him on. He arrived at Port Royal exhausted and delivered his message, which was promptly forwarded to Governor Curtin waiting in desperation at the Capitol. Thence it was transmitted to President Lincoln and thence to General Meade.

Close to the Tuscarora, through all its beautiful course runs a highway recommended to the motorist devoted to beauty rather than speed. Travelers on main roads believe they know the lovely Juniata, but none knows it until he has explored its creeks, crossed its covered bridges and lifted trout or bass from its mountain waters.

The northern tip of Tuscarora Mountain still confronts the placid river but having threaded so many gaps it finds another mountain no hindrance. Gliding past Turkey Ridge, receiving the waters of Cocolamus Creek from the north and

Photo: R. B. McFarland

From the bridge at Millerstown the low wooded mountains press close to the stream.

Through the graceful arches of Juniata Bridge the Juniata flows to its tryst with the Susquehanna under the shadow of Peters Mountain. The distant bridge is the Clark's Ferry crossing of the Susquehanna.

Photo: K. A. Drayer

THE JUNIATA

smaller streams from the south, it slips round new ridges, past pleasant Millerstown and Newport, to Amity Hall and another brimming confluence, forty miles below the junction of the North and West branches. By this time the main river has outgrown the spirit of its youth; now, augmented by the Juniata, it flows at least for most seasons with middle-aged quiet.

Here one must climb one of the many surrounding heights to view the majestic prospect. In the foreground lies Duncan Island, scene of many battles between whites and Indians. Here separated the branches of the Susquehanna Canal, here the Juniata Bridge spans the Juniata. On the far side of the Susquehanna above the eastern end of a much longer bridge, rises the steep cone of Peters Mountain.

Dr. Henry S. Shoemaker has described the river as a loving and observant eye might have seen it long ago.

"Along the Juniata in those days flourished giant buttonwood trees, interspersed with wahoos and red birches. Wonderful beds of reeds grew along the water's brink, affording hiding-places for myriads of water fowl. The wild swan often sailed before the storm when the usually calm waters were churned into a choppy sea by some sudden gale. Great blue herons waded along in the shallows angling for frogs, lizards, watersnakes, and other arch enemies of food fish. The Brown bittern or Indian hen crouched among the swaying rushes. Sometimes the sky would be darkened by the flight of wild pigeons which seemed to rise like a cloud out of the crest of distant Mahantango, a sort of Columbine Vesuvius. At sunset the great line of ruddy pink along the sky seemed an endless infinity of color, so rich that it must dye the river for all time to liquid mother-of-pearl. At night when the young crescent moon climbed over the Tuscarora summits and reflected itself in the calm waters, the peepers, whippoorwills, wood thrushes, katydids, foxes and wolves greeted it with musical incantations from the mountain heights by turns according to the seasons."

Fortunately beauty remains though some of its details are altered. Having motored downstream, the traveler should reverse his course and return to behold an equally beautiful and different scene. In spring sunshine and shadow alternate, long pale willow whips wave in the breeze, laurel blushes on the hillsides, daisies whiten the fields, and the State Highway Department's yellow lilies mark the culverts under which plunge the many springs.

From Blue Hill on the west shore of the river is seen the joining of the North and West branches. Northumberland lies between the two, Sunbury on the main stream to the south.

Photo: Courtesy Penna. Dept. of Commerce

THE MAIN RIVER
NORTHUMBERLAND TO HARRISBURG

> "I have seen
> In land less free, less fair, but far more known,
> The streams which flow through history, and wash
> The legendary shores—and cleave in twain
> Old capitals and towns, dividing oft
> Great empires and estates of petty kings
> And princes, whose domains full many a field,
> Rustling with maize along our native West,
> Outmeasure and might put to shame! and yet
> Nor Rhine, like Bacchus crowned and reeling through
> His hills—nor Danube, marred with tyrany,
> His dull waves moaning on Hungarian shores—
> Nor rapid Po, his opaque waters pouring
> Athwart the fairest, fruitfulest, and worst
> Enslaved of European lands—nor Seine,
> Winding uncertain through inconstant France—
> Are half as fair as thy broad stream, whose breast
> Is gemmed with many isles, and whose proud name
> Shall yet become among the names of rivers
> A synonym of beauty—Susquehanna!"
>
> —Thomas Buchanan Read
> "New Pastoral"

WITHIN THE ARMS of the broad Y formed by the converging North and West branches of the Susquehanna lies Northumberland, a pretty town with handsome churches, comfortable dwellings and thriving industries. Its tall trees are rooted in deep soil. The architecture of its oldest houses is English. Here, for the last ten years of his life, lived Joseph Priestley, discoverer of oxygen and founder of modern chemistry. At peace after years of persecution because of his religious views, he declared that he did not believe that all the world could offer a more delightful situation.

Despairing of the arrival of the millenium in France to which they had looked forward, and also of happiness and a good life in any long-established civilization, Samuel Taylor Coleridge and Robert Southey proposed to establish a community

Susquehanna floods have been especially damaging at Sunbury, shown here during the flood of 1936. Flood walls are now being erected, designed to prevent disaster in the future.

Photo: Official Photo US—AAF

NORTHUMBERLAND TO HARRISBURG

near their friend Priestley. Twenty young couples determined to leave behind all systems of government, religion and education and emigrate to America. The young men were to produce food for the support of the colony and the young women were to do the household tasks. All labor was to be accomplished in a few hours of each day, and the remainder was to be devoted to reading and discussion.

Photo: R. B. McFarland

The flood wall at Sunbury may interfere with the view of Shikellamy Cliff as seen from Penna. 14 along the river.

The promoters could not carry out their plans, and their connection with the Susquehanna was limited to some poetic compositions. Never except in imagination did they see the merging rivers, the imposing hills, the craggy walls of rock, the plunge of spring freshets, the long lines of birds uttering strange cries as they followed the river, now south in autumn, now north in spring.

Today the rounded hills, some of which are still thickly wooded, the steep rock walls, the converging rivers, the passenger and railroad bridges compose a panorama rich in both scenic and historic interest, though inevitably already much that was interesting is gone. Neither the long moan of a conch shell nor the sharp blast of a horn heralds the approach of the canal boats that once made their slow way up the west bank of the main river from Duncannon, down the east bank of the North Branch from Athens and New York State, or eastward on the West Branch from Lock Haven.

Nor do ponderous rafts of logs take the wide curves or little steamers puff back and forth across the river on Shamokin Dam; the little steamers and the dam itself are long gone. The steel and concrete bridges lack the picturesque quality of three roofed and ancient predecessors that extended from the west bank of the West Branch to Northumberland, from Northumberland to the island in midstream and from the island to the east shore. The two that spanned the North Branch were built by the Susquehanna's most famous bridge builder, Theodore Burr, of whom we shall hear at Harrisburg, Columbia and McCalls Ferry. Hills and rivers are little changed, and the play of light and shadow upon them is the same.

From Northumberland and Sunbury it is easy to reach the neighboring heights. From Blue Hill above Shikellamy's profile one may look down into clear water beneath the concrete which at present spans the West Branch and see the massive logs upon which rested the piers of an ancient covered bridge. One may also look down upon other bridges, upon Northumberland among its trees and upon Packer Island dividing the North Branch.

Mile Hill commands an even wider view. Yonder is Sunbury, yonder converge the quiet waters. From the lookout provided by the widened road at the summit of the hill one can tell where the heaviest rains have fallen. The North Branch may be flowing placidly, its color blue or blue-gray; the West Branch is rough, its brown surface capped by lines of foam. For a long distance downstream, the waters of the two may be told apart.

One hears on the heights only faint sounds—the sough of the wind, the bray of a Diesel engine, the eerie, nostalgic whistle of a steam locomotive, the clangor of shifting cars, the fainter, sharper tooting of a dredge bringing from the river bottom some of the diminishing residue of coal.

One may hear in imagination many other sounds—the wolf's howl or the fox's bark against the sough of the wind in giant pines and hemlocks, stiffening against

Photos: *Robert W. Gable*

Throughout its course, the Susquehanna is used for sport and recreation. Here, at Selinsgrove, the successor to the Indian birch-bark canoe is ideal for the broad, shallow stream.

Photo: R. B. McFarland

Penns Creek, entering the river from the west, parallels the Susquehanna, forming a long peninsula—an island at high water—called the Isle of Que, deeded by Chief Shikellamy to Conrad Weiser. From Penna. 14 across the river can be seen the tip of the "isle."

the blast of the tempest. Not all the women and children carried captive into the forest that they expected to be their prison for the remainder of their lives, went quietly—does one hear their shrill wailing? One may imagine he hears also the moan of the conch shell, hollow on the breeze, or the trot, trot of horses' feet on the wooden floors of the covered bridges.

One may believe he sees Iroquois in long canoes or dugouts. They have been visiting the conquered tribes in the valley, or they are returning from errands of vengeance in North Carolina. Here is Etienne Brulé with his Indian companions, here is Lewis Evans surveying for his maps, here John Bartram, awed by the immense trees and enchanted by rhododendron and shadbush. Here are ardent Moravians with hearts hungry for souls; here Conrad Weiser hastens desperately to stay the uplifted hand of the Indian warrior.

Imagination may penetrate still farther into the past. Dense forests cover the hills; their shadowy depths are haunted by wild beasts long since vanished. Bear, deer, enormous elk and bison step cautiously toward the river or crash through underbrush, pursued by the new sort of enemy carrying on his shoulder or horizontally in his hand a long fire-spitting stick. Smaller creatures, skunks or foxes, peer from their dens to be sure that no larger animal watches at their drinking place. Raccoons steal to the river bank or to little streams to wash their food, as is their sanitary custom.

One may picture an immense ribbon of passenger pigeons shadowing the blue water, both its beginning and its end out of sight. The ripples follow the course of a muskellunge; the quick leap is that of a shad. The snaky line marks the course of an eel for which there is as yet no W-shaped trap. These are visions from a past forever gone unless man opens his dams, lets his wood roads close, destroys his firearms, his railroads, his mines.

One may reconstruct a glittering, desolate landscape—ages ago these valleys were filled, these hills overtopped by a blanket of ice a thousand feet thick, now motionless, now advancing, its southern walls melting, rocks and sand from far away settling down to puzzle mankind, the bones of mastodons protruding.

All creatures of stream and forest and sky are not gone. Overhead still speed the wild geese, honking their way north to nesting places in Canada when shad-blow and spicebush bloom. The great hawks and the eagles still soar; with luck

PENNSYLVANIA'S SUSQUEHANNA

and sharp eyes one may identify an astonishing number. Close to the bank swings a wide-winged, long-necked blue and gray heron, his legs trailing. And these white birds, too large for blue herons in their second season—can they be egrets? The answer is yes; their food in South Carolina swamps killed by spraying, they have come north for the summer to safer homes.

From Blue Hill and Mile Hill it is easy to see that no area has more to fear from the Susquehanna floods that tear open the heart of Pennsylvania. The passage between the hills is narrow, and upriver forests no longer delay the plunge of water down the steep slopes; the natural channel of the river has been in some places altered and narrowed. Sometimes, though very rarely, one may look from Blue Hill and Mile Hill upon a lake from which protrude chimneys and roofs and into which vanish railroad tracks and highways.

Those who love the river, even those who are the chief sufferers from floods, prefer not to discuss the hardships they bring. "I am sixty years old and there have been only two bad floods in my time," one will say. "We make too much of them."

There is frequent and fervid argument about flood control. Will upriver dams hold the water? Is it better to build dikes at vulnerable points in cities? Will dikes be effective or will flood waters merely gather behind them? Sunbury is building dikes; Harrisburg is not.

Below the junction of the rivers, upon the site of the original Shamokin, on the east bank stands Sunbury. Here the Iroquois Long House stationed a sachem to rule the tribes they had conquered and to keep a watchful eye on the ever-advancing whites. Here lived Chief Shikellamy. Friendly with the whites, he esteemed especially Conrad Weiser, official interpreter of the Commonwealth, whom he guided on his arduous and important journeys to try to keep peace. Often he stopped at Womelsdorf to take Weiser with him to Philadelphia, there to interpret his suggestions and protests. Let the white men advance no farther. Let them send no more firewater into the forest to deprave the young men. Let them cease to cheat and to rob the women and children of subsistence. A Christian in spirit but a true Indian, he must have grieved bitterly as he watched the moving water and realized that, like it, his people and their ways were vanishing.

Close to the river is partially reconstructed Fort Augusta, erected by the British and named for the mother of King George. Intended as a sanctuary from

122

Again from Penna. 14 where it crosses Fisher Ridge, the approach to Dalmatia gives an extended view upstream.

Photo: R. B. McFarland

NORTHUMBERLAND TO HARRISBURG

Indian attack, it received fleeing and terrified settlers, served as a point of departure for expeditions against the Indians and French, and with its cannon warned away war parties looking down from Blue Hill.

Sunbury, as well as Northumberland, has scientific fame. Selecting the town for experimentation because the cost of gas illumination was excessive and because the fuel for a new sort of lighting was at hand, Thomas Edison, a hundred years after Joseph Priestley's death, set up the first three-wire central-station electric lighting plant in the world. How strangely the bright gleam must have flickered over the dark water!

Shadbush (*Amelanchier canadensis*) in early spring makes a misty haze in the woods.

Photo: J. Horace McFarland Co.

Approaching Dalmatia from the north on Penna. 14, the motorist views the Susquehanna swinging to the west around the bases of Hooflander Mountain and Fisher Ridge.

Photo: R. B. McFarland

South of Sunbury on the east shore, Penna. 14 winds to and from the river and crosses many hills. As here, north of Herndon, many vistas of island and river can be seen.

Photo: R. B. McFarland

NORTHUMBERLAND TO HARRISBURG

Below Sunbury, close to the city and conspicuous in the landscape, rises a new rectangular building with tall chimneys, the natural successor of Edison's lighting plant. Here anthracite coal is transformed into light and power. The coal utilized is not the first run from the mines east of the river, but the culm or waste, long accumulated in mountainous piles. Soil on the river banks is altering visibly from the black of sterile coal to the live brown of fertility. Shamokin and Mahanoy, Mahantango and Wiconisco creeks will each year be less thick with fine dust.

West of the river and east of the highway stand two markers. That on the Albany Treaty line indicates that the land to the east as far north as Oswego belonged to the King of England. The other marks the massacre of German settlers in 1755. Notified by fleeing companions of the slain, John Harris of Harris' Ferry, fifty miles away, organized a company to investigate. Fifteen bodies were found. Thereafter forts protected in a measure the Germans east of the Susquehanna and the Scotch-Irish to the west, who formed the bulwark against the Indians and French.

For five miles below Sunbury the river flows in a wide valley. To the west it is closely paralleled by Penns Creek, which forms a peninsula, once an island, named by French travelers the Isle of Que, from its resemblance to a tail. The property of Chief Shikellamy, it was transferred by him to Conrad Weiser and became the property of Weiser's descendants.

Motoring south on the long street of Selinsgrove, one loses the river. One suspects that some of the old houses were shaded by trees, but the trees are gone. Nearby to the west lies the pretty campus of Susquehanna University with tall conifers and lovely glimpses of the river.

To the east, secluded and almost unsuspected, a section of the town occupies part of the Isle of Que. Once two bridges connected it with the mainland; now there is only one, and over it the "islanders" cross to church and school and shopping. A few streets intersect at right angles. The houses are for the most part unpretentious, but several large brick buildings recall a busy past when Selinsgrove was a canal town, with the boat-builder's hammer continuously pounding and farmers' wagons heavily loaded with produce for Harrisburg or Baltimore, waiting in a long line.

Ahead, after one has crossed the bridge, is a wisely placed sign—Dead End.

Photo: R. B. McFarland

Descending Fisher Ridge from the north, one sees a wide expanse of island-dotted river backed by the mass of Mahantango Mountain.

NORTHUMBERLAND TO HARRISBURG

It would not be strange if on reaching this point the unwarned and startled motorist drove straight ahead. Some have done just that.

Here, unseen until you are upon it, flows the river, for three miles in an almost level course, blue on a blue day, gray on a gray day, an ever-changing mother-

Photo: J. Horace McFarland Co.
Trailing Arbutus (*Epigæa repens*), a sweet-scented but shy woods beauty.

of-pearl if there are light clouds in a sunny sky. Islands close to the east shore diminish the actual width of the water but the open half-mile is broad enough to display all possible variations in the surface, now smooth as glass, now softly rippled, now dappled with whitecaps, now uniform for long periods, now changing each moment.

A few boats are moored before the narrow beach or perhaps moving in the

Photos: R. B. McFarland

A turn from Penna. 14 in Millersburg brings one to the river and the ferry running to the West Shore, as it has for years. Downriver from Millersburg is a wide view through the gap of Berry Mountain.

NORTHUMBERLAND TO HARRISBURG

river, on errands of business or pleasure. The largest craft is a dredge salvaging coal; the others are rowboats or canoes, or possibly a kayak. If the water level is high, a motorboat may rush noisily back and forth, like a duckling first introduced to a pond. When you have parked and shut off your engine and the motorboat has gone, a snowy egret may drift by, or rarely a great blue heron may trail his long legs. A black-crowned night heron, occupying an island with his immense circle of family and friends, may squawk at you. Always there are killdeer running along the shore, and kingfishers, peering from branches that extend over the water, alert for an unwary fish.

If it is springtime, you see yellow jessamine and forsythia cascading down the bank; and if the river has not been too high, spring perennials are abloom in a few sloping rock gardens. The bank is twenty feet high—surely the water does not rise to the streets! In 1936 it rose to the streets and yards and climbed the three or four shallow steps to the doorways and to the second step of the inner stairways.

"And what do people do?" you ask. What hundreds of others do, in other valleys, in Williamsport and Milton and Sunbury and Harrisburg and Columbia. The majority stay where they are. This is not the first flood; it will probably be no worse than others through which the citizens have lived.

All hearken for the Niagara roar under the railroad bridge, the young hoping that it will be loud enough to drown out all other sounds in the world. The sound is unmistakable. "Now!" say the older people. "Now it's here!" Through the branches of a mammoth sycamore torn from the earth the water passes with a strange swishing that has a deep, almost bass undertone. That sibilance will not long continue; soon the tree will go downstream like a giant swimming desperately, first one arm over his head, then the other.

Some older people will watch wide-eyed for the repetition of unforgettable spectacles—sunrise on the turbulent brown current, moonlight banding the torrent with silver. If a flood comes, let it come! Let us not miss this aspect of our river. Let us hurry to the railroad bridge and look and listen—provided, of course, that there are no watchmen to prevent.

All along the river, boys, older and younger, will carry about portable broadcasting machines and announce from areas that have otherwise no communication with the world the need of food or medical service and of motorboats to rescue

The west shore of the Susquehanna is followed closely by US 11 and 15, from which may be enjoyed many intimate water-level views of the river. At Liverpool, there spreads a magnificent panorama of river and mountains. To the

those in danger. Not otherwise, with telegraph and telephone wires down and trains stalled, will news reach the world.

Tucked away on Penns Creek is an easily flooded area called Little Norway. Smooth places for skating on the river itself are often hard to find, corrugated as it is by the current and the wind, unless one knows a sheltered channel between two islands.

South of the Isle of Que, Middle Creek, flowing placidly into Penns Creek, bears no trace of a gruesome tragedy on its headwaters. There, in the last days of the eighteenth century, lingered the buffalo that gave their names to creeks, townships and streams. Descending from the hills in search of food, three hundred, following a great bull to which the settlers had given the name Logan, collected on the farm of Samuel McClellan. Led by old Logan, the herd rushed into the little cabin and in terror milled round and round until they had destroyed McClellan's wife and three children. A hunt was organized and, frantic as those who followed them, the buffalo fled to a distant ravine and there were butchered.

Below the entrance of Penns Creek, the river narrows as it passes Mahanoy

Photo: R. B. McFarland

left Mahantango Mountain and, just beyond, Berry Mountain enclose the Williams Valley. The distance is limited by Peters Mountain. Continuing to the right are the ends of Berry Mountain and Buffalo Mountain.

Mountain. To the east, behind or along the tall ridges cut through by the river or projecting to its very verge continue deep and valuable deposits of anthracite coal. For many years great quantities were carried by rail from Trevorton and elsewhere to the village of Herndon, and from there were transported over a bridge to Port Trevorton on the west shore, to be dumped into canal boats waiting beneath the bridge. Like the ruined locks, the dilapidated piers recall a method of transportation once widespread and important, now forever past and for the most part forgotten.

Mrs. Olive Aucher Glaze describes in the admirable Journal of the Northumberland County Historical Society the noise and fervor accompanying the building of the bridge.

"Raftsmen were floating timbers for trestles, masons fitting and placing stone, divers and engineers locating piers and fixing foundations, engines and derricks puffing and wheezing as they swung materials into place, clinking and clanking noise of unloading iron, blasting rock, teamsters swearing at oxen and mules and horses, engineers shouting orders, foremen bawling out directions, all mingled with

Turn toward the river from US 11 and 15 in New Buffalo and you will find unspoiled river bank. Imagine water in the now empty canal bed with mules pulling a laden boat and you are back to 1850.

Photo: R. B. McFarland

the song of the Irish laborer as he wheeled his barrow, wagon or cart, to and fro.

"All walks of life were represented. Skilled mechanics from Boston, engineers from New York, Yankees from up the river, Irish fresh from the Shamrock Isles, backwoodsmen, hoodlums, vagabonds and stragglers all contributed their bit. They came in all kinds of conveyances; some walking, others riding horses or mules. Farming in the immediate vicinity was at a standstill; all the able-bodied men were working at the bridge or the railroad. Selinsgrove, New Berlin, Liverpool, Sunbury, Freeburg and Shamokin furnished quite a few. Many walked to and from these towns daily. They lived in anything that would shelter them—tents, house-boats, trees, shanties, anything that would hold a bunk. Their meals were cooked in the open, and their evenings were spent in the barroom, drinking, gambling and carousing."

One workman walked the length of the tavern dinner-table, belabored by his fellow workers, who were too befuddled to know whether he were friend or foe.

Mrs. Glaze concludes with a stanza which, following upon the vivid account of the clamor and the flying potatoes and gravy, not to speak of plates and tureens, takes the reader by surprise. Thus, she thinks, sing the waves of the river, as they dash against the ruined piers:

> "Break, Break, Break
>   At the foot of thy crags, O Sea!
>   But the tender grace of a day that is dead
>   Will never come back to me."

One should not, perhaps, be too greatly surprised. Life, however hard and rough, does in retrospect take on a tender grace.

The past shone no more brightly than the future. A typical statement of the importance of the new bridge to neighboring communities, also of the rivalry between river towns for connection with the world, is quoted by Mrs. Glaze:

"We learn that the bridge at Port Trevorton is ready for travel. This is now one of the most important on the Susquehanna River, opening a direct communication with the Trevorton coal fields. It also affords to the traveling community a crossing place during the winter season, and when the river is at such a state that persons cannot cross the ferries. We have no doubt that this bridge

Photo: R. B. McFarland

The tip of Peters Mountain forces the main Susquehanna to its most westerly point. Here, at Juniata Bridge and Clark's Ferry, the Susquehanna is joined by the Juniata. From this point, US 22 goes south on the east and US 11 and 15 south on the west bank of the river.

will and must eventually be the main crossing for all the travel to Pottsville, Reading and other places, while on the other hand, it gives to the farmers an advantage to obtain coal at a much lower price than heretofore. To make this bridge an advantage to Port Trevorton and to the traveling community generally we must at once have a direct route from Middleburg.

"Should this road be made, it would be of a vast deal of benefit to Port Trevorton, and would necessarily throw all the travel from the western part of the state through Middleburg, and would also give our farmers the double advantage of selling their produce at advanced prices while at the same time they could get their coal from seventy-five cents to a dollar cheaper than they do now. Port Trevorton and Middleburg are both deeply interested and their interest being one and the same, an effort should at once be made to have the road opened.

"Remember, too, that Selinsgrove is straining every nerve to get the county-seat; that, once obtained, the next great effort will be for a bridge, for which they have a charter now. The bridge would be death, both to Middleburg and Port Trevorton. Now is the time for the two latter places to act in unison. You have a common enemy, who are seeking their own advantage; why shall you lie idle and not seek yours?"

Swinging west round Hooflander Mountain and Fisher Ridge, the river receives two tributaries of the same musical Indian name—Mahantango. That from the west is a clear stream separating Snyder and Juniata counties; that from the east, which is darkened by coal dust, separates Northumberland from Dauphin.

Opposite Hooflander Mountain lies a rocky ridge called McKees Half Falls. Its western end, extending over half the river, consists of two ledges, together five feet high. McKee was a famous trader, who, it is said, remained at his post when another settler was driven away by the loud noise of the rapids, the clamor of his neighbor's cowbells and the smell of shad from the fishery on one of the islands. The roar of the rapids has long since diminished, cowbells are no longer heard, and as for the shad that were once caught as far north as Tioga Point, their ascent has been blocked since the first cross-river dam was built, and a profitable industry ceased to be.

The eastern Mahantango enters opposite a thickly islanded area. Summer's reeds give the wide spread of water a swamp-like appearance, but the stranger

At Clark's Ferry, the river crossing of US 22 is a handsome concrete arch bridge, copied by the bridge over the mouth of the Juniata.

Photo: K. A. Drayer

NORTHUMBERLAND TO HARRISBURG

who comments in disappointment upon the shallowness of the channel, perhaps repeating the ancient jibe that the river is a mile wide and a foot deep, should return when the radio warns that the water is rising. Then islands disappear and the long reeds vanish or appear to float on the surface, only their tips visible.

Almost constantly in sight beside the highway along the west bank, runs the ditch that was once the Susquehanna Canal. Stones neatly ranged one upon another are set into the grassy bank or lie in heaps half covered by vines or bushes. Between the partly filled and grassy depression a thin growth of trees, chiefly water birches, enhances the lovely pageant of the wide stream, now approaching a gap between hills with almost perpendicular walls, now curving to create the appearance of a lake. Tall, scantily limbed locusts suggest the pillars of sylvan temples, Greek in design, but with a brilliant drapery of Virginia creeper that is American and not Greek.

In spring wild roses flourish, pale and lovely, and elderberry and honeysuckle perfume the air, even to the motorist as he speeds by. In autumn sumac deepens to maroon, sometimes veiled by silvery clematis. All are projected against the blue stream, which deepens or pales according to the density of the leafy screen.

South of the entrance of the two Mahantango creeks rises Mahantango Mountain, which appears to have as many different profiles as there are points of the compass, the most impressive being a huge hump viewed from across the river. The hump, which vanishes mysteriously when seen from north or south, seems to shove the river to the west and the long town of Liverpool into the bank. In Liverpool, as in other river towns, one must leave the street that carries the main highway and descend to the water's edge to reconstruct the activity of past days. Here the excellent coal from the Lykens Valley was brought from east of the river and the mountains and transferred to canal boats.

More than one artist has found inspiration in the wide stream and the picturesque hills, and if he narrows the stream, gives the mountains a still more noble elevation and veils all with mist, that is his privilege. If he has recorded for us hills and streams and canals and canal boats now altered or gone, we may be doubly willing to forgive modifications in the interest of beauty.

For long distances there is hardly a mile where the river is not visible from the highway on the west side. Across the reedy islands from which a heron or an

As the road rounds the shoulder of the north spur of Cove Mountain, south of Duncannon, there opens a broad view of river, here running almost due east. Between riffles dredges salvage river coal, washed from North Branch collieries.

Photo: R. B. McFarland

egret may soar, the tall ridges rise at right angles to the river. Some the river appears to have cut through; others cease to be at its bank, with no extension on the opposite side. The jacket of Dr. Myers' "The Long Crooked River" pictures this not always realized aspect.

Between the ridges lie farmlands, bright with wheat's springtime green or summer's yellow ripeness or dark with tall corn. The channel widens, then narrows and the river and mountains become more majestic with each mile. The sensitive traveler is aware of a sort of suspense. Passing between the mighty bastions into the widening water, he wonders whether the ocean is at hand. But the ocean is still far away, and ahead many other hills face one another endwise.

The water flows at a slow pace, hardly hiding the rocky bottom, then with rapidity that warns boatmen away. The motorist drives to the side of the highway in order to look back. All is changed; perhaps the scene is less majestic, perhaps more—at any rate it is not the same. Viewed a second or third time to north or south, it is still not the same.

Opposite another half-falls, the rocks of a perpendicular cliff have been named, not for a benevolent, intelligent Shikellamy but for Simon Girty, a renegade from his race who is supposed to have hidden in a cave on the hillside. Drummed from a Virginia regiment because of misbehavior, he thereafter allied himself with the Indians and neglected no opportunity to be revenged upon his own race.

The red and rocky walls here and wherever they are seen along the river, exude moisture from springs above and behind them and are tapestried with delicate and lovely flowers—Dutchman's breeches, harebells, bloodroot, wild geranium. In many places there are maidenhair ferns, and in winter clumps of a low and sturdy variety with leaves that are not killed by cold. Fortunately flowers and ferns are well out of reach of the longest arms.

The highway on the east bank does not always command a view of the river, but as it crosses the mountain ridges it provides more dramatic views that have the added quality of unexpectedness. The Halifax Cemetery, seen from far downstream, is planted with tall arborvitæ that carry one's memory to Italian landscapes set with statuary and cypresses. From the town itself one looks upon a broad expanse broken by large islands named for pioneering settlers.

The "brave little Juniata" slips into the river at a sharp angle. The point is cut by a channel that divides it lengthwise into two islands, Duncan's and Haldeman's, both interesting to archeologists because of the skeletons and artifacts found in their soil.

David Brainerd, the veteran Presbyterian missionary, sadly reported the Indian inhabitants hopeless in their heathenish behavior. At first he was encouraged to think that his preaching might have some fruit, but on a second visit he was profoundly shocked and depressed. In the evening the Indians gathered round a large fire, prepared to sacrifice ten fat deer. Setting the fire blazing with the fat of the intestines, they danced and shouted. The next day they gathered again while their conjurers tried by juggling and tricks to diagnose the wasting disease that afflicted them all. "In this exercise they were engaged for several hours, making all the wild, ridiculous distracted motions imaginable, sometimes singing, sometimes howling, sometimes extending their hands to the utmost stretch and spreading all their fingers, sometimes spurting water fine as mist; sometimes sitting flat on the earth, then bowing down their faces upon the ground; then wringing their sides as if in pain and anguish, twisting their faces, turning up their eyes, grunting and puffing."

Surely no traveler along the river was ever more depressed than the godly minister to whom the beauty of the hills and the river was no compensation for the disappointment of his hopes. His health broken, he departed to return no more.

The painter or photographer collecting views of the river is likely to have his heart broken by the many that he must reject. Never will the fracture be deeper than here. Whether he looks north or south, east or west, he is enchanted. To the east rises the rounded end of the ridge called Peters Mountain; round its base canal and railroad and highway have carved rights of way by months and even years of difficult engineering.

A noble and easily accessible view may be had from the Presbyterian Cemetery at Duncannon, now obscured somewhat by a school building. The adult should find compensation for the loss of a part of the magnificent prospect which the pupils have ever before their eyes. Our forefathers may have selected the sites of cemeteries such as this because here the graves were far above the danger of flood. Or it may have been for the consoling beauty. When in the long ago the first dead were laid in this spot, their friends, looking across the wide empty river at the green

Photo: R. B. McFarland

Penna. 225 from near Halifax to Dauphin offers a short-cut over Peters Mountain. As the road descends the south side of the mountain, the distant Susquehanna appears as a mountain-girt lake, reminding travelers of the lakes of Scotland.

The southern arm of Cove Mountain and the Second Mountain on the east form the gap at Dauphin Narrows, here seen from a platform on the fire tower along US 22.

Photo: R. B. McFarland

mountain wall may well have found it impossible "to imagine unquiet slumbers in the quiet earth."

Beneath, the housetops of Duncannon are thickly shaded by trees; yonder bridges cross the two rivers. The school-children may not know of the immense covered bridge over the Susquehanna at Clark's Ferry with its turnouts for passing teams, or the aqueduct that once carried the canal across the Juniata, but they may enclose for themselves one noble view after another, using the perfect arches of concrete for frames.

From its source to its mouth travelers crossed the river first by fords, then by ferries. In time residents along the banks provided transportation and shelters where travelers on foot or mounted might find or summon a boat and boatman. A single canoe or boat might make the crossing, or two lashed together. As the river widened, rafts or flatboats were propelled by broad cars or sweeps, and heavy loads were conveyed. Where the current was strong, the boat was attached to a cable and thus drawn against the force of the water. Not only human beings were transported but animals and large vehicles, even the enormous, heavily laden Conestoga wagons originating in Lancaster County.

Clark's Ferry, the most northern of the long ferries, established by Daniel Clark in 1785, had temporarily various owners and names but never lost that of its original owner and conductor.

A striking view of Duncannon may be found in "Picturesque America," the collection of engravings and descriptions edited by William Cullen Bryant. The angle of view is carefully selected or invented. High over the peaks of the mountains rides the moon; from the iron furnace rise the bright flames of waste gases burning at the bleeder. The molten slag gleams as it rolls down the high dump.

Below the Juniata two lovely streams, Sherman and Conodoguinet creeks, besides others of less length or volume, flow into the river from the west. On Sherman Creek took place savage Indian attacks. One was upon a family whose head invited a company of Indians to sit at his table and was informed that the intruders came not for food but for scalps. These they at once proceeded to secure.

The Conodoguinet is distinguished for curves surely unmatched in number in any stream. It rises in Franklin County and flows north, for a while closely parallel to the Conococheague, which flows south into the Potomac. From Carlisle

Where US 11 and 15 rounds the end of the south spur of Cove Mountain on the west bank, the rocky river is dotted with islands. Stretching east and west, this is a favorite spot to see a summer sunset.

Photo: R. B. McFarland

A spring river-bank hillside of native Phlox (*P. divaricata*).
Photo: O. P. Beckley

the distance to Harrisburg by road is seventeen miles; the lovely curves of the Conodoguinet measure sixty. Some of the areas almost enclosed by its meanders appear to be islands. Both the streams and their little tributaries are crossed by covered bridges.

Journeying southward from Clark's Ferry Bridge and the entrance of the Juniata, the traveler may choose between two routes and make no mistake. He will find that on the east bank straighter and more traveled; that on the west commands the more varied and beautiful views. If he chooses the west bank and a wind from the east suddenly darkens the sky and clouds his eyes with smoke and steam, he must drive carefully, reminding himself that he is looking down upon Enola, the distribution yards of the Pennsylvania Railroad, largest of their kind

The Rockville Bridge of the Pennsylvania Railroad is the longest stone-arch railroad bridge in the world, carrying the four-track main line across the Susquehanna.

Photo: H. B. Herman

in the world. If there are small boys in the car, perhaps a little weary of scenery, they will cry, "Slow down! Slow down!" If the driver heeds, he will soon quicken his pace, so long is the distance from end to end.

He will need in a moment another superlative. Here is the Rockville Bridge, said to be the longest stone-arch railroad bridge in the world. To be appreciated in its full beauty it must be viewed from the south. It seems to rest on the water, and the long trains lose weight and substance. To the north a tall ridge apparently extending from mountain to mountain closes the distant horizon, itself a perfect horizontal. Like the bridge, wooded islands appear to lie on the water. Having at hand this reach of the Susquehanna, no one need sigh for Maggiore or Isola Bella.

When the ridges of the Alleghenies vanish and their lovely blue no longer bounds the horizon, it is not the ocean that comes into view but the city of Harrisburg, capital of the Commonwealth of Pennsylvania, located, as most cities are located, not for the sake of beauty but of business. Downstream to the fur-trading post of John Harris, established in 1719, floated Indian canoes, carrying heavy cargoes of pelts from the upper river and its tributaries. The supply of furs of northern Europe was being depleted; in America, untouched except by the Indians, waited the fur-bearing inhabitants of immeasurable and unexplored forests— bear and deer, wolves and foxes, beavers and martens.

Not only to Europe but to Asia were shipped the skins piled in canoes under the high bank before John Harris' cabin. Outside his storehouse hunters bargained in guttural tones for what they believed was a fair exchange in guns and gunpowder, mirrors and beads, cloth and whiskey, the last to be one of the chief causes of their destruction.

Soon white hunters or pioneers who intended to farm accompanied the traders from the seacoast; they too would share in the wealth of the wilderness. Crossing the river individually in canoes, then in flatboats on which they could transport their pack horses and articles for trade, the hunters entered the forest. Presently the boats ceased to be poled but were drawn by ropes. At each terminus a roof was provided to shelter the travelers as they waited for the slow return of the ferry from the other side of the river. Drought, too high water or ice might delay their departure for hours or days.

Some of the newcomers, chiefly the hunters traveling alone or in small groups,

Photo: R. B. McFarland
From the Dauphin County shore, Marysville nestles beside Cove Mountain.

went directly westward into the forest; those that brought their families to establish homes turned south on the long road down the Cumberland Valley where jutting gray limestone and towering walnut trees indicated fertile soil. All looked amazed and many terrified at the wide river and the forest, so dark and dense and still. A company of crows cawed, or a tree fell, not with a loud crash but with a soft swishing as its branches caught on those of its neighbors. Disturbed as they might be, few turned back. They had burned their bridges, and there was nothing to do but go on.

Each hunter and settler who crossed the long ferry complicated a little more the relation of Indian and white. Uneasy, the whites ceased to wait at Philadelphia for the Indians to come to them with gifts or petitions, but dispatched agents deep into the Indian country. Across John Harris' Ferry southwest to Carlisle, and thence far west to the confluence of the Allegheny and the Monongahela, called the Forks of the Ohio, rode ambassadors to confer with the Indians on matters not only of land or trade but of life and death.

NORTHUMBERLAND TO HARRISBURG

Trains of pack horses followed them, heavily loaded with presents. Upon the success of their journeys depended the holding of the land against the French pouring down from Canada to meet their fellow countrymen coming north from the lower Mississippi. Conrad Weiser had traveled the trails along the North and West branches to placate the Six Nations; now he crossed at Harris' Ferry to visit Carlisle and the Forks of the Ohio, and to be warned by his Indian friends that the high wind of war was rising.

In 1794, only seventy-five years after the Indians began to spread their pelts of beaver and mink and fox on the earth before John Harris' trading post, President Washington drove his traveling coach down the steep east bank of the river and across the ferry. It is not impossible that a few Indians lingered about, perhaps to be near the grave of Chief Tanacharison, who was John Harris' friend. What incredible changes they and their river had watched! A few decades in the

Photo: R. B. McFarland
Through an arch of the Rockville Bridge toward the distant York Hills.

151

Just north of the city of Harrisburg lie the first two gaps where the Susquehanna flows through the Blue Ridge Mountains. The Rockville Bridge extends the line of the first ridge of mountains on the north side of "the Great Vale of Pennsylvania."

Photo: R. B. McFarland

past and this was their land; now strangers poured in like the waters of the Susquehanna in flood.

President Washington was traveling much farther into the forest, his errand concerned with the authority of himself and the Congress. The new nation must levy taxes, and in the southwestern corner of Pennsylvania lived stubborn men who would pay no tax on whiskey. Corn, the pioneer's best crop, was easy to distill and its distillation easy to transport; why give away part of the profit upon it?

He must have looked with delight upon the river and the hills. The time was early October. On gum trees and Virginia creepers leaves were reddening. The broad river, he must have thought, promised to be a great route of trade. He had seen many rivers, and this river in other places. Nowhere was it more beautiful than here. Since the rebellion was already weakening, he needed to go no farther than Bedford. Returning by way of a southern route, he visited the future site of Harrisburg no more.

The almost incredibly rapid penetration of the wilderness is indicated by Dr. John T. Faris in "Old Trails and Roads in Penn's Land," one of his many valuable accounts of the past. He quotes the *Oracle of Dauphin and Harrisburg Advertiser* of June 6, 1798:

"Last Friday crossed the Susquehanna, near this town, on their way to the President of the United States, sixty-three Indians and seven Squaws, having in their custody a white prisoner (charged with having murdered one of their chiefs), whom they were to demand of the President in order to sacrifice according to their custom (pine-knot splinters and the stake), and agreeable to treaty."

Nine years later, in 1807, a historian painted another picture:

"It was not at all uncommon to see as many as five hundred packhorses passing the Harrisburg ferry, going westward loaded with seeds, salt, iron, etc. The iron was carried on horseback, being crooked over and around the bodies of the animals; barrels or kegs were hung on each side of this. These faithful packhorses were generally placed in divisions of twelve, carrying about two hundred pounds each, going single file, and managed by two men, one going before on the leader, and the other in the rear to see to the safety of the pack. When the bridle road passed along declivities over hills, the path was in some places worked out so deep that the pack or burden came in contact with the ground, and was often displaced."

PENNSYLVANIA'S SUSQUEHANNA

Dr. William H. Egle, editor of "Notes and Queries" in which are gathered many items of Pennsylvania history, mentions other ferries, including Maclay's at the upper end of Forster's Island opposite the city, Lytle's just below Berry Mountain and Clemson's at Fort Halifax. To the south were Chambers' and Skeer's.

Not always would travelers be content to paddle or pole across the river or be drawn by a rope. Drought, ice or raging freshets made these methods of transportation uncertain or unsafe. In October a traveling coach might be safely lowered on one bank and raised on the other; but during some months the transfer from shore to flatboat would be perilous.

Far upstream, when General Washington crossed at Harris' Ferry, there were short bridges, but none spanned the river at its greatest or nearly greatest width. Urged by public demand, the Legislature of Pennsylvania in 1809 incorporated companies and authorized the construction of bridges at McCalls Ferry, Columbia, Harrisburg and across the North Branch at Northumberland. It was then that Theodore Burr offered himself as architect and builder. A native of Connecticut, later a resident of Oxford, New York, he had already proved his ability by spanning the Hudson at Waterford and the Delaware at Trenton.

The bridge from Columbia to Wrightsville seems to have been the first of the four, according to Richard S. Allen, who has accumulated all discoverable material about Burr, and then the bridge at McCalls Ferry. The bridges at Northumberland and Harrisburg followed.

Longest lived of the four was that at Harrisburg. Portions endured for more than a century, and one original section is remembered by many now living. The stains of time are said to have mottled the roof like a snake's skin. The roof rose and dipped in strange curves like those on the back of a camel, and by that resemblance it was known. It was called, not "the camelback bridge" but "the camelback" as though that designation were sufficient.

Burr purchased standing timber along the Chemung River and floated it downstream. Living on Front Street, he had his river almost as a dooryard. After a while he built a house on Forster's Island, which was crossed by his bridge. From here he could see the long wings sweep right and left.

The bridge was divided lengthwise into four sections, the two on the outside for foot passengers, the two within for carriages, wagons—hundreds of covered

Photos: R. B. McFarland

Of all Pennsylvania cities, the capital city of Harrisburg has made the most of its river front. Front Street parallels the Susquehanna for five miles with a park of varying width between the highway (US 22) and the stream. The entire length is a changing scene of loveliness.

On the north end of Forster's Island, Harrisburg maintains a public bathing beach, open to all and used by thousands. The distant mountains and river islands lend beauty to the site.

Photo: The Hill Studio

wagons among them—and domestic animals on their way to market in the Harrisburg Square. Once enclosed in the central section, the animals could be counted and the toll reckoned.

Burr's biography is not finished at Harrisburg or with the camelback; downstream where the mighty flow of the waters enlarged and quickened came the climax of his daring and adventurous life. The known incidents are comparatively few; some may still be discovered in newspaper files not yet searched, bank vaults not yet visited or private letters not yet unfolded. The hope that his portrait might be found was quickened by the discovery that a Burr married a Catlin, but so far it has not been proved that the limner of Indians painted his contemporary and neighbor in the center of Pennsylvania.

In 1812, Harrisburg was made the capital of the Commonwealth, and from the distant forests and counties near at hand came the Governor and his staff, representatives of the people to make and execute the laws, and all who had business with the Commonwealth of Pennsylvania. Here, in 1861 assembled thousands of boys to defend their nation from division and destruction. Hundreds tramped the long bridge, not too weary perhaps to make the rafters ring with directions to rally round the flag or assurance to Father Abraham that they were on their way. Most of them no doubt were elated and excited. Here was the broad river of which they had heard from their fathers, which their grandmothers and grandfathers had crossed. They were on the famous camelback, one of the wonders of the age; they were free from the obligations of home, they would see the world. They would be given military flags, but the flags made by loved hands were dearer and they would bring them proudly back. No one could know that more than four years would pass before that day came.

Charles Dickens, who did not like all Americans or all American ways and who crossed the camelback in the evening on his way to embark on the canal, describes it in unforgettable phrases. It was almost dark, and as the horses attached to an enormous stage ambled toward "the distant spark of dying light" the length of the bridge seemed interminable. It was, he said, "perplexed with great beams, crossing and recrossing at every possible angle."

Mr. James Cameron, grandson of Simon Cameron and son of Donald, both famous Pennsylvanians, remembered the confusion of beams overhead and the clat-

PENNSYLVANIA'S SUSQUEHANNA

ter of the carriage-horses' feet. "My father tried to guide the horses and it made them uneasy," he said. "My grandfather let them take their own heads, and they were not disturbed."

The bridge lost some of its sections in floods and some by fire. For a time they were replaced and it retained a part of its picturesqueness. In 1902 the last section was swept away. Completed in 1817, the bridge had survived for eighty-five years the heat of the summer sun, the moisture of long rains and the buffeting of gigantic missiles of ice propelled by a rough and powerful current.

"It will not stand!" said many in 1817, as they watched the building of the piers.

"It has stood eighty-five years!" said their great-grandsons in 1902.

The Susquehanna is Pennsylvania's river, but it is especially Harrisburg's river. In the same way Harrisburg is the Susquehanna's city. Its towers, domes

Photo: The Hill Studio
The Harrisburg river basin is used extensively. Kipona is a yearly Labor Day sports event sponsored by the city.

Photo: R. B. McFarland

On the Cumberland County side of the river, Memorial Day Boat Races are sponsored by the West Shore Aquatic Club.

and spires dominate the scene; some are higher than the hills. The first Capitol was surpassed in height by a few church spires; now the massive structure that houses the administrative, executive and judicial offices of the Commonwealth appears lower than some of the buildings in its neighborhood. The great buildings are here because of the river, as the Capitol is here because of the river.

No longer are passengers ferried from bank to bank; no longer do the feet of horses send a loud thunder rolling through the Stygian darkness of the ancient camelback. From the city two railroad bridges and two bridges for passenger and vehicular traffic swing across the river. Gasoline and oil transport hundreds of thousands. Whither do they go? The answer is—to the ends of the earth.

Looking down from the dome of the Capitol or from one of the heights of Reservoir Park or the high lands on the west side, one sees a close-built city, extended in every direction by suburbs, some on low land close to the river, some on the steep banks. Lengthwise lies Forster's or "*the* island," as though there were no other in the world. Once it was the abode of eagles, which, having soared high, fell upon the shad leaping from the water. Eagles may be seen now by the sharp-eyed, and those of duller vision may rejoice in the flocks of migrant fowl enlivening the sky or lingering overnight in spring and fall.

The island is the city's playground. It takes a mother's care of children who wade and bathe; it provides ample space for football or baseball. It has rowboats and canoes to rent, and for a small consideration the light-hearted were once admitted to a large boat upon which they might dance. Beside the river lies a sunken garden and not far away a rose garden named for Dr. J. Horace McFarland, chief among the promoters of beauty for Pennsylvania's citizens.

The views from the heights are no lovelier than the views from the river level. To come suddenly from a narrow street on a spring day is a never-to-be-forgotten experience. The river is seen through veils of blossoming crab or cherry in the long park. Slow-moving dredges are bringing up fine coal, which forms pyramids on the flatboats trailing behind them. Boys and girls paddle or row happily. If a motorboat speeds noisily, the lover of quiet prays that it go home, and soon the prayer is granted. Motorcars and trains form a moving border on each bank, but they may be ignored in the vast space of river and mountain and sky.

In "Picturesque America," a few paragraphs describe the view above Harrisburg:

"From the cupola of the Capitol not only can one survey all the city with its climbing spires, its massive manufactories and their aspiring chimneys, but the bold scenery to the northward comes into view and one has a distant though most beautiful view of Hunter's Gap and the range of mountains through which the Susquehanna has to fight its way. There are no less than three ranges, tier upon tier standing out in bold relief against the sky, each having a different range of blue. Escaping from these the river bursts as with a frenzied joy and from the imprisonment of its sandstone walls widens its bed prodigiously and makes a tremendous sheer to the west before it strikes due south. Hence, opposite Harrisburg, the river is unusually wide . . . In the center of the sheer which the river makes is the pretty village of West Fairview. Straight in line from the glittering cottages of the village, are three islands of a size that picnics are possible on them. They are very close together but there is a pass between them through which shallops can

NORTHUMBERLAND TO HARRISBURG

glide . . . It is glorious to be here . . . in summertime . . . when the sun sets behind the ranges of mountains . . . The haze that wraps their forms is turned into a haze of supreme glory, and the last rays come shooting through the commingled foliage like veritable arrows, and fall upon the water in long pencils of reflected fire. These grow more dusky and dreamy, until they become only faint blotches of dim light . . .

"In the meantime there has been a battle between the golden haze and the blue upon the mountains. At first the gold carries everything before it, save at the bases which seem mantled in a brilliant green. This spreads until it covers all the mountain forms and then it slowly, slowly changes to its accustomed blue and the bold crests of the ranges hidden by the wealth of golden fire show vividly against the clear pallor of the twilight sky."

Sailboats at Harrisburg Kipona.

Photo: The Hill Studio

The Pennsylvania Canal north of Harrisburg about 1900. Generally tree-lined, these man-made waterways had a beauty of their own. Too few of them have been preserved to show the mode of transportation in common use a century ago.

Photo: O. P. Beckley

CANALS, STEAMBOATS AND PIRATES

"Navigating the Susquehanna is very much like dancing 'the cheat.' You are always making straight up to a mountain, with no apparent possibility of escaping contact with it, and it is an even chance up to the last moment which side of it you are to *chassez* with the current. Meantime the sun seems capering about to all points of the compass, the shadows falling in every possible direction, and north, south, east and west, changing places with the familiarity of a masquerade. The blindness of the river's course is increased by the innumerable small islands in its bosom, whose tall elms and close set willows meet halfway those from either shore, and the current very often dividing above them, it takes an old voyager to choose between the shaded alleys, by either of which you would think, Arethusa might have eluded her lover.

"A friend of mine took it into his head that as salmon and shad will ascend a fall of twenty feet in a river, the propulsive energy of their tails might furnish a hint for a steamer that would shoot up dams and rapids. A Connecticut man undertook it—the product of his ingenuity was the steamboat Susquehanna, drawing but eighteen inches, having beside her sidepaddles an immense wheel in the stern which playing the slack water of the boat would drive her up Niagara, if she would but hold together. I think she had made three trips when she broke a shaft and the canal was half completed between her two havens before the experiment succeeded."

—N. P. WILLIS

THE TRAVELER along the Susquehanna will be able to trace for most of the distance from New York to Maryland, from Bellefonte and Williamsport to Northumberland, and from Hollidaysburg to Duncannon a ditch closely paralleling the river. For many miles it is a shallow, grass-grown depression. Where water has gathered, there are beds of rank grass, of cat-o'nine-tails or calamus. Quaker ladies and bouncing bet, white ageratum and asters of many shades follow one another in bloom. Thickets of elder, sumac, alder, spicebush, dogwood and redbud form a foreground planting for a taller growth, especially of water birches, scant of foliage on their lower trunks, half hiding the river and heightening its beauty.

For mile upon mile a railroad seems to take the place of the ditch, and the unobservant visualizes no long, carefully engineered depression beneath the tics and rails. Here and there close to the river stand large old buildings too far from the highway to have been designed as shelters for motorists, too dilapidated to serve as comfortable tenements. Old piers lie in ruin—they are not quite like the piers

Canal lock at Market Street, Harrisburg, about 1900, showing the way in which canal boats were raised or lowered from one level to another.

Photo: O. P. Beckley

CANALS, STEAMBOATS AND PIRATES

of bridges. Here is a sign "Aqueduct"—did an aqueduct cross the Juniata River? What purpose did it serve?

If you are so fortunate as to encounter an old man gazing sadly at a bit of ruined masonry, question him and hope that he will not be too contemptuous of your ignorance. "That ditch? Why, that's the canal! Aqueduct? Why, that was a wooden box that carried the canal and the boats across the Juniata."

In 1787, the vast Northwest Territory was opened to settlement. Adventurer after adventurer, explorer after explorer brought back tales of great forests, fertile land and an abundance of wild life. Each new discovery made the problem of transportation more insistent. How convey inland the citizens to whom the Atlantic seaboard seemed crowded? How bring to eastern markets the products of the West?

William Penn had proposed a canal across Pennsylvania. Robert Fulton declared that the time would come "when canals shall pass through every vale, wind round every hill and bind the whole country in one bond of social intercourse." In 1817 at Rome, New York, was begun the Erie Canal, largest, most famous and most successful of all similar enterprises. Eight years later the canal boat *Seneca Chief* carried the Governor and a company of notables from Buffalo to New York City. It carried also a cask of Lake Erie water that the Governor presented to the mayor of New York, who thereupon completed the ceremony by pouring the water into the Hudson.

Pennsylvania woke swiftly to her consequent loss of business. Like one of the Susquehanna's own floods swelled the demand for a canal system that should carry freight to Philadelphia and thus restore the enormous and profitable trade that New York was taking away. Dependent upon high water, requiring almost superhuman strength, transportation on the river was perilous and uncertain at best. The rafting or floating of logs downstream was one matter; the steady carrying of wheat and corn and the manufactured products of wood was another.

The Susquehanna drained the sources of some of this great wealth. Why not parallel her course with a canal? It was true that in the Allegheny plateau Pennsylvania had a barrier more stubborn than any in New York. A Susquehanna Canal could go thus far and no farther. But on the west side of the plateau a canal might follow the Kiskiminitas, and a connection could surely be devised.

PENNSYLVANIA'S SUSQUEHANNA

In 1825, every county in Pennsylvania sent delegates to a canal meeting in Harrisburg. A railroad from Philadelphia to Columbia was designed as the first link in the route across the state, and upon the rails would move not only cars but boats mounted on wheels, to be eventually launched on the canal.

Rapidly surveys were made and promptly excavation began. The canal was to parallel the east bank of the river from Columbia to Clark's Ferry. There the propelling power, otherwise horses and mules and their drivers, would cross a bridge, towing the boat. Over the Juniata at Amity Hall boats would move in an aqueduct, and from there the canal would lie now on the south, now on the north bank as space and curves permitted. At Hollidaysburg passengers and freight would be transferred to cars and carried on five planes up, and then on the same number down the Allegheny Mountain, to be transferred to the Kiskiminitas Canal.

The route planned became the scene of furious activity. Five thousand laborers were employed, many of them recently imported Irishmen. All known tools and machinery for excavation were provided—shovels, plows, scoops and material for blasting.

Where roads crossed the river or a valley provided a natural shipping point, towns sprang up. Lewistown, which had been a village, rapidly increased in population to two thousand; Hollidaysburg matched it in growth because of the large business of transporting passengers and freight over the mountain. Presently the boats themselves were hoisted up the steep grade and lowered on the far side.

North of Clark's Ferry the canal continued up the west bank, now hugging rocky cliffs, now bordering wide meadows on which the river had for centuries deposited fertile soil. At Northumberland it swung northwest beside the West Branch. Here, where millions of feet of lumber from one direction and thousands of tons of coal from the other seemed to flow together, where other products of the two great valleys awaited shipping, canal activity was most concentrated.

The lumber business had promoted the establishment of settlements at Williamsport, Jersey Shore, Lock Haven and other places. To all towns situated on the river, canal traffic continuing regardless of high or low water brought about a further expansion.

From Northumberland the North Branch Canal paralleled the river as far as

Photo: Henry Troth

A pleasure trip on the Juniata Canal in 1883. The canal boat *Comfort* traveled from Harrisburg to Huntingdon and return. Time, two weeks.

Athens, where it joined the Junction Canal connecting it with the Erie Canal. The names of many of the promoters are forgotten, but one name is remembered— William B. Foster, Jr., a canal engineer, brought his brother Stephen to live with him at Towanda and attend the Athens Academy. Athens historians, ever mindful of the treasures of the past, cherish the tradition of the little boy, especially the fact of his writing here his "Tioga Waltz."

Canal building did not end with excavation. Locks of substantial masonry and varied design must be constructed; wooden gates must be swung and machinery provided for their opening and closing. Houses must be built for lock tenders, houses and stores for laborers and inns for patrons, weigh-houses for loaded boats, bridges for travelers on foot or in vehicles, basins where boats could be built, others for the storage of boats. Sometimes banks collapsed under their own weight and had to be reinforced with stone or clay.

PENNSYLVANIA'S SUSQUEHANNA

In all, four hundred miles of waterways accompanied the river and another four hundred its tributaries. Some were financed with State funds, others by private capital.

No famed author has set the plots of novels and stories against the background of the Pennsylvania Canal or any of its romantic branches, as Walter D. Edmonds has in the case of the Erie Canal. The Pennsylvania Canal has, however, its historians. In 1842, Charles Dickens continued west with his wife, her maid and his valet, and a large assortment of luggage to see America. He was in a critical mood, especially and with good reason, because of the pirating of his works by American publishers and because of the prevalent use of tobacco in its most unpleasant form.

Leaving Harrisburg for Pittsburgh on the canal, he recorded in his "American

Photo: Courtesy Historical Society of Dauphin County
A section of the Pennsylvania Canal where it traversed Dauphin Narrows.

CANALS, STEAMBOATS AND PIRATES

Notes" much that was undoubtedly obnoxious. A dirty boat, wretched meals, beds that were merely shelves on the wall, no privacy, no facilities for bathing, the not inexcusable astonishment with which his fellow passengers regarded his elegant clothes, all combined to make him uncomfortable. Yet he saw beauty and grandeur.

"Even the running up, bare-necked, at five o'clock in the morning, from the tainted cabin to the dirty deck; scooping up the icy water, plunging one's head into it, and drawing it out, all fresh and glowing with the cold, was a good thing. The fast, brisk walk upon the towing-path, between that time and breakfast, when every vein and artery seemed to tingle with health; the exquisite beauty of the opening day, when light came gleaming off from everything; the lazy motion of the boat, when one lay idly on the deck, looking through, rather than at, the deep blue sky; the gliding on at night, so noiselessly, past frowning hills, sullen and dark trees, sometimes angry in one red burning spot high up, where unseen men lay crouching round a fire; the shining out of the bright stars undisturbed by noise of wheels or steam, or any other sound than the limpid rippling of the waters as the boat went on: all these were pure delight.

"Then there were new settlements and detached log-cabins and frame-houses, full of interest for strangers from an old country; cabins with simple ovens, outside, made of clay; and lodgings for the pigs nearly as good as many of the human quarters; broken windows, patched with worn-out hats, old clothes, old boards, fragments of blankets and paper; and home-made dressers standing in the open air without the door, whereon was ranged the household store, not hard to count, of earthen jars and pots.

"The eye was pained to see the stumps of great trees thickly strewn in every field of wheat and seldom to lose the eternal swamp and dull morass, with hundreds of rotten trunks and twisted branches steeped in its unwholesome water. It was quite sad and oppressive, to come upon great tracts where settlers had been burning down the trees, and where their wounded bodies lay about, like those of murdered creatures, while here and there some charred and blackened giant reared aloft two withered arms, and seemed to call down curses on his foes. Sometimes, at night the way wound through a lonely gorge, like a mountain pass in Scotland, shining and coldly glittering in the light of the moon, and so closed in by high steep hills, that there seemed to be no egress save through the narrower path by which we had come, until one rugged hill-side seemed to open, and shutting out the moonlight as we passed into its gloomy throat wrapped our new course in shade and darkness."

A participant in a very different canal trip was Dr. J. Horace McFarland, famous and beloved Pennsylvanian. In 1883 he journeyed in summer with a company of young people pleasure-bound from Harrisburg to Huntingdon. The boat, which had painted on its side *Comfort of Harrisburg*, was clean, the company congenial and gay. The mules that furnished the motive power were called Jinny and Puss. Cherries and mulberries were ripe, fields were yellow with wheat. If rain descended, the travelers remained under cover playing games or writing verses. The rising of the water under the boat at the locks, the splendid sunset seen across the Rockville Bridge, the ever-changing view of the mountains that opened and closed before the slow-moving craft, all were recorded. The travelers dived from the deck to swim, or found exercise in walking the towpath or climbing Blacklog Mountain. Fish came quickly to the hook. A rattlesnake furnished excitement; the fierce refusal of a village postmaster to hand over mail after closing hours, emotion of another sort. On Sunday progress ceased. Truly a record of a happy, leisurely and far-off day! Incidentally, the forty years that had passed since the expedition of Dickens and his party had elevated the standard of travel, and the young people on this expedition carried their own cook.

Volume XVI of the Proceedings of the Northumberland County Historical Society is made up largely of articles about the canal. William A. Schnure describes a trip from Northumberland southward, through locks, into slack water, past a log boom, round shady bends, past Liverpool and Montgomery Ferry, Amity Hall, Clark's Ferry, Rockville, Harrisburg, Steelton, Falmouth and Bainbridge where there was a deep lock called the Hogpen, and finally round towering Chickies Rock to the end of the canal at Columbia, where connection was made with Philadelphia.

It has been said that the Susquehanna is lovable, boatable, dammable but not navigable. This estimate is not a matter of offhand judgment but has been arrived at with considerable loss of property and some life. Charles A. Fryling has combined in an article in the same Volume XVI of the Proceedings of the North-

Photo: Courtesy Historical Society of Dauphin County

A canal boat being towed through the lock at Dauphin.

umberland County Historical Society the record of history and his own recollections of steam navigation on the river.

Maryland, first to see the importance of the Susquehanna as a highway, expended large sums for the removal of rocks from its lower course. In 1771 the Pennsylvania Assembly declared the Susquehanna and several tributaries public highways and from time to time appropriated money for the opening of the channel.

Steam navigation was discouraging from the start. In 1812 a vessel of twelve tons, built at Wilkes-Barre, went aground at Conewago Falls. In 1825, the *Susquehanna*, built at Baltimore, succeeded in journeying to Danville on the North Branch and Milton on the West Branch. A small sheet-iron steamer, the *Codorus*, constructed at York Haven, ascended the river to Binghamton and reported navigation by steam impracticable. In 1836 either the *Susquehanna* or a namesake was de-

PENNSYLVANIA'S SUSQUEHANNA

stroyed by the explosion of her boiler at Nescopeck Falls. Four persons were scalded to death and others injured.

By this time, as the canal was begun and dams built to serve as feeders, steam navigation was abandoned except in one area. The Shamokin Dam at Sunbury provided a wide sheet of navigable water. For fifty years boats had been operated by poling, ropes or a horse treadmill. Now every half hour steam-propelled ferryboats crossed the river. Mr. Fryling has recorded their names: *Shad Fly, Arrow, Sunbury, Amanda, Empire, Empress, Louis, Rover, Queen, Water Witch, Inverlochen, Ivanhoe, Grant.*

In 1904 the river froze to a depth of almost two feet, and when the ice went out it carried with it a portion of the dam and left the little steamers in ruin.

Now a new fuel speeds the pleasure seeker over short distances in boats of shal-

Photo: *Courtesy Historical Society of Dauphin County*
The Canal Terminal at Columbia just prior to the abandonment of the Pennsylvania Canal.

CANALS, STEAMBOATS AND PIRATES

low draft. Steam still propels the paddles of the dredges that lift waste coal from the river bed, but elsewhere steam navigation has followed the towpath mules.

Also in Volume XVI of the Northumberland County Historical Society Proceedings, Dr. Lewis Theiss describes the rough and sometimes desperately wicked character of many who came to work on the canal and remained to prey upon the boatmen in the lonely and wild regions. Settlements along the river were few and sometimes miles apart, and many stretches of the West Branch and the Juniata were uninhabited. Boat crews fought one another and stole the property of the farmers along the route under the eyes of its owners. Leaping from the low bridges that spanned the canal, brigands attacked bare handed or with clubs or knives, and the attacked defended themselves with axes.

Doctor Theiss makes the interesting suggestion that eventual improvement in behavior was due to the coming of women who journeyed with their husbands or sometimes ran their own boats. Piracy, white aprons, and flower pots in canalboat windows did not seem to belong together.

The canal did not satisfy the expectations of its promoters. The reason for its gradual decline was neither the enormous expense and the incommensurate return, nor the rapid and faulty construction that necessitated constant repair and rebuilding, though these conditions prevailed. The enemy threatened from without rather than from within. The beginning of the canal was the railroad that moved its freight and its very boats from Philadelphia to Columbia. Its central portion was a railroad—on tracks and propelled by steam, the boats surmounted the Allegheny Mountain. Soon the railroad proved swifter and more efficient as a carrier. Except in extraordinary seasons it was not, like the canal, blocked by ice. Eventually it diverted both patronage and interest, and the Pennsylvania and the Philadelphia and Erie systems became the owners of the "long ditch" that had been a source of pride for more than half a century.

Harrisburg, capital of Pennsylvania and county seat of Dauphin County, lies where the Susquehanna, flowing from northwest to southeast, crosses the Great Valley, which runs roughly at right angles to the river. The site is one of great beauty, with the stream passing the city in a gentle curve, and the mountains of the Blue Ridge beyond, broken by the river gaps. A dam provides a pool of constant depth for the water front. Between the first two bridges is the site of the ferry established by John Harris, the trader. His son, John Harris, Jr., laid out the first settlement, which has grown to the present city.

Photo: Penna. Aerial Surveys

THE MAIN RIVER
HARRISBURG TO THE MARYLAND BORDER

"Born by the upper Susquehanna, I had played in its rapids, speared, skated, canoed and sung—down to where it dulls with mine-dust and spreads mile wide to brawl monotony with the dog-tooth rocks; always wondering how this geologically unreasonable stream ended. And here in sunrise on a champagned September morn I saw with homing emotion the prow of a timbered island between wooded hills, the final current slow and inexorable for marriage with the great Bay."

And looking back—"Four hundred miles that shining ribbon stretched upwards by easy grade, through Allegheny gaps, by infrequent steaming cities, proud and decrepit villages, alluvial farms and summering places—to drink of Catskill springs and the shining lake of the Deerslayer."

—Frederic Brush
"Walk the Long Years," 1946

FOLLOWING FRONT STREET southward on the east side of the river, the traveler is suddenly in another world. He passes beside the fenced-in grave of John Harris and under the bridges that carry two railroads across the park and the river. Suddenly the river is lost or screened by miles of great structures—blast furnaces, steam plants and shops, transformers, hoists and cranes of the Steelton plant of the Bethlehem Steel Company. Among the pyramidal heaps of coal and ore, limestone and coke, wind railroad tracks. There is continual clamor of iron on iron, of air under pressure, of hissing steam. Yet all is orderly; in this fashion an expert housekeeper would arrange her belongings.

In a number of Susquehanna tributaries solemn rites of baptism are observed. At Steelton on Twelfth Night, or January 6, the river was formerly the scene of a picturesque ritual of the Macedonian Bulgarian Church. A cross was thrown into the cold and frequently icy water. After it dived the young athletes of the parish, each determined to win the honor of rescuing the symbol of his faith.

The highway runs beside the old canal, still important here at least, and on the other side in tall loops races a pipe that carries water from the canal to the plant, a giant snake from which there is no escape. Only from an airplane can one see the immense plant and even then only partially. From Highspire on the east bank to a rough wooded slope on the west bank stalk the tall piers of

Approaching Harrisburg by rail from Baltimore and Washington, the traveler, at New Cumberland, sees arched river bridges and the skyline of the city against the backdrop of distant mountains.

Photo: K. A. Drayer

the bridge that is to carry a section of the four-lane Turnpike soon to be completed from Pittsburgh to Philadelphia.

At Middletown, Swatara Creek enters from the east, its springs rising in the most southern ridge of the curving Allegheny Mountains, which the geographers call the Kittatinnies and those who live nearby, the Blue Mountains. Into Swatara Creek with brightening hopes turned Conrad Weiser and the German refugees who had found in New York State a cold welcome. They were bound for Tulpehocken, the valley with a turtle-like shape that gave it its name. It is the belief of one student of their journey that their dugouts may still lie deep under the earth along the little beach where they ended their travels. Today in Tulpehocken live their children's children to the seventh or eighth generation.

While building a bridge across the Swatara near its mouth, there died, at the age of fifty-one, the chief builder of Susquehanna bridges, Theodore Burr. No one knows whether accident or disease ended his life. His physical strength and endurance must have been far above average, and only one of temperate habits could have accomplished his arduous work. It is possible that a misstep plunged him deep into the swift current.

Nor does anyone know the place of his burial. It is not likely that his funeral would have been farther away than Harrisburg, but neither at Harrisburg nor at Northumberland, both of which were his homes at various times, is there a record in any cemetery or church.

At least one anecdote about Burr is preserved. When he was building the bridge at McCalls Ferry, he was annoyed by the continued advice of a minister who held services nearby. Presently Burr issued a call to a prayer meeting on an island in the river, and there preached a sermon. When the minister reproached him, he answered, "You preach henceforth and I'll build my bridge."

The river will no longer cut at right angles through mountain ridges, but its picturesque travel is not past. Below Middletown it spreads to almost double its width at Steelton and curves south among a multitude of islands, some visible in all their length, others veiled by thin growth along the bank. On a map of large scale the river seems to be divided into a fringe. The flood plain to the east is occupied by the spreading storehouses and airfield of the army.

Hill Island, which alone is elevated more than a few feet above the water, was

At Steelton, south of Harrisburg, the plant of the Bethlehem Steel Company lies along a rather straight stretch of river extending to Middletown. Across the river, at the right of this aerial view, are buildings of the Marsh Run Army Depot.

Photo: Penna. Aerial Surveys

the scene of an extraordinary demonstration not confined to its small summit. Hundreds of Baptists and others after careful study of Biblical prophecy decided that Christ was to return to the earth in 1843, and multitudes of deluded followers dressed in white robes and waited on elevated land for the miraculous event. Many sold their property and neglected to cultivate the soil or to put out crops; what was the use when the end of the world was at hand? In 1844, Miller, their leader, persuaded them to keep vigil once more, but this was again in vain. To the imagination of some who drive Route 230 the flutter of white is still visible among the sparse growth on the little hill across the river. Is it a waving robe or an uplifted, beseeching hand that catches a ray of moonlight?

Apparently sluggish and lazy, this is one section of the river that presents to strangers a disappointing shock. The shock would be of a different character could they see it broad, swift and formidable, threatening property and life in flood. A few miles of loitering, and its width narrows and its current quickens.

Charles Dickens, driving north to Harrisburg from York, made note of a beautiful area, which the highway has now abandoned for the hilltops. "Our road wound through the pleasant valley of the Susquehanna; the river, dotted with innumerable green islands, lay upon our right; and on the left, a steep ascent, craggy with broken rock, and dark with pine trees. The mist, wreathing itself into a hundred fantastic shapes, moved solemnly upon the water; and the gloom of evening gave to all an air of mystery and silence and greatly enhanced its natural interest."

At York Haven on the west shore originated speculations of wealth almost as unfounded as those that fixed the imminent end of the world. Across the river runs a rocky ridge that seemed the single obstacle to all the hopes of those who believed the Susquehanna to be navigable. In 1795 they constructed a canal around its western end. A town sprang up, flour mills were built, lots were sold. York Haven, its residents expected, would be one of the great cities of the Commonwealth, if not of the nation. In a summer hotel General Lafayette was a guest on his way from Baltimore to Harrisburg in 1824.

Hope of great fortunes lasted for about twenty years, not only at York Haven but in the neighborhood. Farms were divided into town lots and sold at fabulous prices. Soon came the inevitable crash, induced partly by the building of the canal on the opposite side of the river.

From a hill above Marsh Run are seen the buildings of the Army Depot with the river bridges and Harrisburg beyond. Steelton and the Bethlehem Steel plant are just across the Susquehanna. Out of sight at the base of the hill runs the eastern extension of the Pennsylvania Turnpike for a river-crossing just south of Marsh Run to Highspire on the eastern shore.

Photo: R. B. McFarland

HARRISBURG TO THE MARYLAND BORDER

Charles Weathers Bump in a valuable little volume, "Down the Historic Susquehanna from Otsego to the Chesapeake," published in 1899, makes the following observation:

"Some of the waterfall of York Haven is to be used by a company to furnish extensive electric power to the city of York. Similar schemes for harnessing the Susquehanna are being talked of at several other places, including Columbia and Peach Bottom. From the last named place it is expected to transmit the power to Baltimore and Philadelphia."

The York Haven Dam has long been a picturesque reality. A wall of heavy stone crosses the river from the west bank to Haldeman Island, the island itself continues the breast and from there to the east bank a ridge of rock completes the dam. The generators are on the east side and the transformers on the west. Power is supplied not only to neighboring towns but to a paper mill.

Not everyone approved the building of dams across the river. Lloyd Mifflin, a resident of Columbia and one of Pennsylvania's most skillful and best loved poets, expressed his sorrow and regret.

> "Farewell, ye wooded islands, never more
>   Shall in your shade the Youth and Maiden woo!
> Ye rocks, that jutted from the rushing blue,
>   Within whose eddies dripped the lover's oar,
> A last farewell! Ye currents that of yore
>   Like maddened horses furious dashed, and threw
> Your white manes to the air, farewell to you!
>   Forever mute your danger-luring roar!
>
> "Here, as I drift, no rapture doth awake
>   From hills or moving landscape, for my heart
> Lingers beneath where I was wont to roam;
>   And memory sees, as on some sunken chart,
> Down in that inert bottom of the lake,
>   The scarred old boulders yearning for the foam!"

To others the building of the dams meant the exchange of darkness for light, of labor for a measure of ease. At York Haven there is less change of scene than in the environs of the larger dams downstream.

PENNSYLVANIA'S SUSQUEHANNA

You do not see the whole of any river by studying its surface from the bank. Now it has a mirror-like smoothness, now it is rough, now delicately rippled. Nor does a view from a boat or an airplane reveal its details. Beneath it lies a bed that may be hard or soft. Perhaps as on the Susquehanna above Sunbury, a glacier may have proceeded on its slow and destructive way. Perhaps its melted ice flowed in Niagara rushes that hollowed out deep gorges. Perhaps boulders carried by icebergs or ice floes have ground deep pits. In October, 1947, thousands of visitors made their way to the foot of the ridge at York Haven to see the curious and fantastic forms into which the hard rock had been carved. No doubt many were glad when rain fell and the potholes were filled and the tortured rocks again covered from view.

One of the scientists who took pleasure in the strange sight was Dr. Herbert H. Beck of Lancaster, Director of the Franklin and Marshall College Museum.

Photo: R. B. McFarland
At Royalton, across Swatara Creek from Middletown, the Susquehanna is broad and, at times, placid.

Below Royalton, a slight rise on Penna. 441 again shows the broad river with Middletown in the distance. Hill Island, one of the few islands of the Susquehanna with any elevation, rises at the left.

"What is probably one of America's most extensive displays of a singular geologic phenomenon—the deeply bored and sculptured igneous rocks of a river-bed—was uncovered in its entirety the third week of October, 1947, for the first time in the memory of man, when the drought-parched Susquehanna River retreated far beyond its normal 'low' stage and exposed a fantastic wonderland of Nature's tremendous and never-ending handiwork.

"The prolonged drought of September and October had brought to view a natural exhibit which geologists of Pennsylvania, and of the nation, had not known before. It had never been reported to science.

"The Conewago Falls are caused by a formation of Triassic diabase or trap rock, a sill of which, a mile wide, crosses the river-bed between Lancaster and York Counties . . . This sill, often at places a dike, had come up from below during the Triassic Period about 200,000,000 years ago, as a molten mass, to cool far below the surface into crystalline diabase, which throughout the centuries had

From Cly, in York County, just above York Haven, the Susquehanna is seen broadened to more than a mile and dotted with several large and numerous small, low-lying islands.

Photo: R. B. McFarland

HARRISBURG TO THE MARYLAND BORDER

been exposed and brought into its present form by a prolonged and persistent process of erosion.

"Throughout its many million of years in its present course the Susquehanna has been carving potholes and grotesque forms in these diabase rocks and on their floor of the same material. The swirling currents of the rapidly flowing river have

Photo: *The Lancaster Newspapers*
Fantastic formation of the river bed at Conewago Falls. See text.

carried sand, pebbles and boulders which have bored and carved the underlying rock into the usually cylindrical holes known as potholes.

"In the exposed river-bed at Conewago Falls, in an area of about three-quarters of a square mile, there are thousands of these potholes. They vary in diameter from two inches to more than six feet. Some of the larger ones are more than ten feet deep. While most are circular, with diameters increasing in depth, some, through action of counter-currents, are oval or even trough-shaped. There are

Photo: R. B. McFarland
At Bainbridge on Penna. 441, the Susquehanna, calm after passing Conewago Falls at York Haven, resembles a broad lake.

grotesque forms carved and pillared in the boulders like Gustave Doré's fantasies. There are broad sheets of the floor-rock that are carved like undulating waves. In most of the great potholes are the rock-tools that carved them.

"These potholes at Conewago Falls are not unique in the Susquehanna. Below the Holtwood dam, in Drumore Township, Lancaster County, on and about the islands there, for a distance of about four miles, there are scattered potholes, bored in the chlorite schist rock. Some of these attain to ten-foot diameters. Up river, as at Wilkes-Barre, there are even larger ones. But the Conewago Falls pothole formation differs from others in Pennsylvania by the greater hardness of the rock in which the borings and carvings were made—diabase being one of the most resistant of all rocks—and by the larger size of the general formation. It is doubtful if, anywhere in America, there are so many potholes and carvings, within a similar area of about three-quarters of a square mile, as there are at Conewago Falls."

HARRISBURG TO THE MARYLAND BORDER

As York Haven recalls past dreams, Marietta recalls past activity. Old and handsome houses stand on the highest of the natural terraces rising from the river level. Here some of the rafts from upstream were divided into their long timbers, and boats were constructed for river and canal.

Conewago Creek west of the river is much longer than its namesake to the east. The western stream drains the hills of South Mountain and the apple-growing townships of Adams County. The parallel Codorus to the south flows through rich farming land surrounding the prosperous and important city of York. The spires of many York churches are English, as is its name, but its inhabitants are for the most part of Pennsylvania-German origin. Here in 1778, after the British had taken possession of Philadelphia, the Congress met for nine months.

On the west bank, southward from the entrance of Conewago Creek at York

Photo: R. B. McFarland

From Billmeyer, below Bainbridge, is seen the arched bridge of the low-grade freight line, which crosses here to avoid rising hills on the west shore.

Photo: R. B. McFarland

Only rough roads reach Accomac, a summer colony of York County. A series of wild glens rises into the hills to the southwest. In the distance may be glimpsed the railroad bridge, previously seen from Billmeyer.

Haven, a series of ravines cuts through the wooded ridge that borders the river. Most wild and dim of all is Wild Cat Glen, doubtless well named. Through another glen flows Accomac Creek; at its foot and close to the western end of Anderson's Ferry, much used in colonial days, is an inn built from the piers of a railroad bridge long since destroyed. On the river's length there are few opportunities to dine quietly and in view of a wide space of beautiful water.

Highway 241 passes the base of immense and impressive Chickies Rock round which the river turns briefly east. The stiff climb will repay the young and active. To north and east lie the famous farming lands which for many years made Lancaster the most productive county not only in Pennsylvania but in the nation. To the south the river appears to be closed by a shining bridge, white when the sun shines upon it. The space is so vast and the misty distance so vague that at times, as above Harrisburg, the river becomes a lake. The whistle of a train far beneath the summit of the rock is heard as a sound of nature.

Gradually, as one waits, staring, chin on hand, appear a few figures, dressed in the skins of animals, their own skins bronze, with ornaments fastened to their hair—perhaps the feathers of the great bird that they worshipped—all with bows and arrows ready to hand. Sometimes they paddle swiftly as though their business cannot wait, or as though an enemy follows close behind. Presently, coming from the east, a white man climbs the high rock and looks longingly across the river.

White men come to build houses and bridges, finally to lay railroad tracks. The Indians are no longer hunted, but black men are hunted, escaping across the line that divides free from slave country. Wherever there is a Quaker there is a refuge and help on the way, and the river becomes a guide and a highway.

The white concrete bridge extends a mile and three fifths from Columbia, named when there was hope of making the little town the capital of the nation, to Wrightsville, named for the first ferry owner. It proves in a nearer view to overshadow a railroad bridge, a successor of one of the four covered bridges that the Legislature directed Theodore Burr to build, which was destroyed by flood. The second bridge was set on fire by the Union troops so that Confederate forces should not be able to join General Lee at Harrisburg. Perhaps the river has witnessed no more fearful sight, certainly none more terrifying to the inhabitants of its banks. A few days and the thunder of Gettysburg justified the destruction.

From Penna. 441, south of Marietta, a rough road leads to Chickies Rock, a cliff some two hundred feet above the Susquehanna. To the left are the wooded hills of York County. The town of Marietta lies to the right on the east bank of the river.

Photo: R. B. McFarland

HARRISBURG TO THE MARYLAND BORDER

There are no seasons when a visit to Chickies Rock is not interesting, but there are two that bring a thrilling reward. Beside the rock the wide space of water is a flyway where migrating water birds rest on their long journeys north or south. The ornithologist comes in early morning to identify them, some flying in line, some in wedges—river gulls and swans, canvasbacks and redheads, pintails, mergansers, perchance a cormorant or a peregrine falcon—only an ornithologist can name them.

There is another occasion, fortunately not annual, when a climb to the summit of the great rock is worth while. Rain may pour, hour after hour, like the rain of the tropics, as in 1889. The ice that binds Dunning Creek in western Pennsylvania, or Pine Creek or the Sinnemahoning in the north, may melt too rapidly under a spring sun, as in 1936. The wind from the west may waft eastward an unduly large proportion of the raindrops falling on the Allegheny Mountains. The bed of Starrucca Creek may widen, the junction of the Chemung and the Susquehanna become a lake. Springs that seemed to vanish on the steep flanks of Tuscarora or Shade Mountain pour into the Conodoguinet; meanders of the Yellow Breeches unite in one channel. A thousand brooklets become creeks, creeks become rivers.

Then is the time to look from the summit of Chickies Rock upon what the Almighty can do. One should say rather what man can do, because the reckless and suicidal stripping of the hills is his work. In 1936, the pouring rain that thickened the atmosphere above the rising gray-brown waters seemed to turn back the clock of time. Houses disappeared, railroads were undermined, heavily loaded cars rolled down embankments. There is nothing to be seen but rushing water, nothing to be heard but the sound of water. Is this the end of the world? But man is let off easily; in the morning the waters are sinking and the birds flying south.

He who loves a river, especially this river, will sometimes walk across the Columbia–Wrightsville Bridge. It is no doubt a wise precaution against a wandering eye that the walls of the new bridges are made solid so that views upstream and down are limited to the remote distance that can be seen above the rail. Northward the river is at its old trick of cutting squarely through the hills. South there is misty water without bounds. Sometimes the distance is palest white, sometimes blue or rose or gold. It is hard to see where one fades into the other, or where the colors of the sky meet their reflections in the water.

Photo: R. B. McFarland

Above Wrightsville, from the York County shore, Chickies Rock appears as a low hill. The Susquehanna, calm-looking at low water, can be awe-inspiring in this narrow rocky stretch at flood time.

HARRISBURG TO THE MARYLAND BORDER

From the present Columbia to the present Wrightsville extended the most important Susquehanna ferry. Dr. Faris quotes from an earlier observer:

"In the frontier days, all matters of importance were centered at this point on the river. It was the point at which all news of the West was authoritatively handed over to the public authorities. It was the chief watch tower on the river where advice was given as to the coming of Indian movements. It was the place where expeditions West made their first rally and base of supplies for all projects into the new and undiscovered sunset land. It was the Waterloo of Maryland invaders. It was the edge of the woods where the horse-thieves of the southwest found sufficient officers of the law to arrest them. It was the place where the wealth of skins and furs was unloaded when brought out of the virgin forests, where the Indians had been cheated after being treated to firewater. It was the outlying forest where the reign of law met the reign of terror."

Dr. Faris repeats also the description of Robert Sutcliffe, who mentions not only the high rocks that form the banks and the islands that dot the river but the numerous boats and rafts bringing from far upstream the harvests of grain and timber: "I saw a number of large flat-bottomed boats, some of which had come upwards of 300 miles and could carry 1,000 bushels of wheat. The largest are more than seventy feet in length, but calculated for one voyage only, and for floating down the river over shallows and falls; for when they arrive at their place of destination, they are taken in pieces, and the timbers used for other purposes. Besides these boats which have frequently a kind of cottage upon them in which several persons are accommodated during the voyage, there are also many larger floats of timber which are so fixed together as to appear like one large compact body; on one of them a small dwelling house is built for the accommodation of a family. These floats sometimes contain several thousand feet of timber which are conveyed in this way several hundred miles at very trifling expense."

Here was grain from the fields of the upper Pennsylvania counties bound for Baltimore markets or perhaps to be reloaded for Philadelphia or New York or even for cities across the ocean. Here also were the immense timbers from Bradford or Susquehanna counties, the gorge of Pine Creek or the banks of the Moshannon. Today the watcher at Columbia or Wrightsville, viewing the long bridge crossed by thousands of cars in a day, sees nothing more dramatic or in-

PENNSYLVANIA'S SUSQUEHANNA

teresting than the long rafts of logs guided by sweeps in the hands of lumbermen from the remote forests. The low-county men would hail them with a shout and the rafters answer with a yell or a song, possibly about the Lushbaugh girls.

To see Long Level, originally euphonious Conejohela, where for five miles the Susquehanna and Tidewater Canal lying close to the river required no locks, you should visit first the lofty bluff below Wrightsville, occupied usually by a herd of friendly and valuable cattle that do not resent approach.

The lover of beauty sees far beneath the bluff the wide space of water reflecting the clouds. The historian sees that and more. Yonder, best viewed through a glass, lies a little plateau, perhaps green with spring wheat, perhaps brown with corn ready for harvest. Here, he knows, the plough has turned up fragments of pottery made centuries ago, arrowheads, a tiny candle once used in mass in a French

Photo: R. B. McFarland
From Columbia, a beautiful more-than-a-mile-long bridge carries the Lincoln Highway (US 30) across the Susquehanna to Wrightsville.

Photo: R. B. McFarland

South from the water front at Columbia, the first of the rough hills of the lower Susquehanna appear.

church. Evenly spaced round the field, he knows also, are postholes of a stockade now recognizable by the fragments of wood charred to preserve it from decay. Here was a Susquehannock fort, its inhabitants massacred by their enemies the Iroquois, in 1675.

He imagines also two lines meeting at right angles on the little field. West of the vertical line and north of the horizontal line, which is the fortieth parallel, was French-claimed land until 1687. He recalls that a little distance downstream Thomas Cresap, a Marylander, claimed property on the west shore and three beautiful islands that he defended from a fort. As fiercely as Pennsylvanians and Connecticut men fought one another for possession of the Wyoming Valley, Pennsylvanians and Marylanders fought for the possession of southern Pennsylvania, given by the British king to both Pennsylvania and Maryland.

There may be a sail on the river, or the slow-moving rowboat of a fisherman, but the historian, lingering, sees instead a canoe or dugout hugging one bank or

Traveling south from Wrightsville on Penna. 624, turn into Lauxmont Dairy Farms where, from the hilltop, spreads an extended view overlooking the Indian Conejohela, now Long Level, so called because no locks were needed for a long stretch

the other as its fierce passengers make their way home to Onondaga, the Long House, far, far away.

When you drop down to the level of the river, you pass many pleasant cottages before the road swings you away. Again you wish for a scenic highway and again you realize the difficulties of its engineering. Also you are instantly thankful that these ravines remain unspoiled so that present and future generations may climb through them, awed by the stillness, amazed at beds of mertensia and columbine and the pink-white clusters of rhododendron.

To see to best advantage the second of the power dams foretold by Mr. Bump, you go south on the east side of the river. It is not located at Columbia, where he expected it to be, but at Safe Harbor. Columbia, a busy town when the Pennsylvania Canal unloaded its passengers and freight or transferred its boats to the

Photo: R. B. McFarland

in the Susquehanna and Tidewater Canal. In the distance, across the Susquehanna, can be seen the fat farms of Lancaster County, one of the richest agricultural counties in the United States.

Susquehanna and Tidewater Canal, was busier still when the shops of the Pennsylvania Railroad were located there. The highway that parallels a maze of railroad tracks and giant conveyors for electric power lies sometimes on a level with the river and sometimes beneath the embankment that carries the tracks. Beside the highway stand houses that seem to have been built in another age.

The river is presently wholly out of sight but your hopes are sustained by many signs: "Safe Harbor! Safe Harbor! Safe Harbor!" painted in white on a red ground, embellished by the zigzag lines that can have but one interpretation—the source of light next in power to the sun must be at hand.

At Turkey Hill, to be ascended only on foot, the river narrows as though a fist were driven into it, and doubling in almost human fashion, swings southeast. The Conestoga Creek, rich in beauty and history, enters, broad as it is, almost unseen

From the village of Long Level on Penna. 624, the Susquehanna begins its rapid drop to tidewater. Now on calm water at the head of a ten-mile pool above the Safe Harbor Dam, this was once a treacherous stretch of "white water." Across the river is the headland of Turkey Hill and, just beyond, Star Rock.

Photo: R. B. McFarland

because now the roadside signs still bearing the graph for lightning, read "Observation Point!"

So near is wild country that as your car climbs the hill a deer may cross your path. You have time for a shock of surprise but little else. Another moment and you find yourself in close proximity to a dozen or more tall straddling steel towers set in orderly ranks, and you look far over a wide lake.

When you have stared long toward the north, and have taken a deep breath you look directly down—at the power house and dam, extending from bank to bank, at the locomotive, dwarfed to the proportions of a toy, moving slowly on a track enclosing the intake. Trains move under the hill; possibly you hear the murmur of machinery in the long power house. No sound is louder than the sigh of the wind or the scream of a jay or the sharp cry of a gull.

You turn your head to look south. Below the dam the water is shallow; far away the river vanishes around long wooded slopes, less steep than the mountains upstream. A fisherman is unloading his gear on a rocky island. If he wears a red shirt, you see him clearly, but if he is dressed in dun-color, as fishermen are more likely to be, you are not sure that he is a man, or that he moves. Possibly he knows nothing of the day when the ownership of an island-fishery made a man rich.

He may pull in a few catfish of several varieties, carp, perch, sunfish, suckers, eels or chubs, but none of the ocean fish—shad, white perch, rockfish or sturgeon, abundant far upstream before the power dams blocked their journeys. In the Franklin and Marshall College Museum there is on exhibition a sturgeon four feet long, taken above Marietta about 1860. In the words of the Director, "the sturgeon, large of size, easy to spear, must have been prized food for our long-lost friends who named Conejohela and Conodoguinet."

A few workmen on the hilltop may regard you with interest. The foreman has time to answer your questions. "Yes, it's a great dam." "Yes, those towers in the valley carry light and power to towns and cities." "Yes, these towers up here are lightning arresters. At the power house, someone will explain everything to you; you'll understand then how water is changed into light." Oh, will we? "You're welcome to fish from a boat upstream or down, or from the dam itself." He may wonder why we do not follow his advice but instead stand staring as though we drank a long draft and the bottom of the glass were still far, far away.

199

High above the dam and power house at Safe Harbor, the Pennsylvania Water & Power Company has provided an observation point where visitors can enjoy the rugged beauty of this part of the lower Susquehanna valley.

Photo: R. B. McFarland

HARRISBURG TO THE MARYLAND BORDER

As the historian and archeologist see more than a long level of smooth water when looking down from the bluff below Wrightsville, so they see more than a smooth lake and a power dam as they look down upon Safe Harbor Dam. Among the submerged islands lies Walnut Island, once covered by the tall trees that gave it its name. The trees were felled at last and the island turned into a farm. When one of the owners cut a race across it in order to supply water for a mill, the river and especially the river in flood had its destructive way, now uncovering the rocks, now blanketing them with silt, now washing the silt away.

On the uncovered rocks various persons observed incised hieroglyphs or, more correctly, petroglyphs; and before the dam was allowed to fill, scientists under the direction of the State and with the assistance of the Pennsylvania Water & Power Company spent months in making models of these petroglyphs. The inscriptions, so ancient that the Indians of William Penn's day could not interpret them, bear interesting resemblances to picture writing of other races long gone.

Not only were petroglyphs recorded but bowls, plates and other specimens of pottery were rescued and preserved. Graves were opened and many bones and one complete skeleton unearthed. In the State Museum and also in the museum at Safe Harbor may be seen some of the recovered articles. A bulletin of the State Museum describes the sometimes perilous process of their recovery.

Another sort of hieroglyph has been found in the river valley in the neighborhood of the Conodoguinet and the Yellow Breeches creeks. On stones of various sizes, deep grooves and strange lettering have been engraved. Dr. W. W. Strong of Mechanicsburg, who has made a study of these odd objects, believes the writing to be Phoenician in character and cites various journeys of the Carthaginians to the west. This would be indeed a curious and mysterious footnote to the history of our Susquehanna!

The writer who declared the scenery dull to the south below Columbia had obviously never visited that area. Few Pennsylvanians realize that between Columbia and the bay the river falls two hundred and twenty-five feet. Many know nothing of the three power dams in Pennsylvania and one in Maryland that use four times over the same Susquehanna water to produce light for their houses and power for their machinery and some of their railroads. They may have seen the tall towers that carry wires across the country, and they may have wondered

Photo: K. A. Drayer

In York and Cumberland counties, along the Susquehanna, have been found curiously incised stones whose markings, here emphasized in black, suggest characters of the Phoenician alphabet. Scientists who have collected these stones have connected them with ancient Phoenician writings telling of a fair land to the west, thus suggesting the presence of Old World settlers in this region before the Christian Era.

HARRISBURG TO THE MARYLAND BORDER

vaguely about the course of the Susquehanna in southern Pennsylvania but they have not gone to explore. Descending to cross the Conowingo Dam, which is also a bridge, they may glance swiftly at the large area of water above—a lake, is it? They remember no such lake in their geographies.

At Columbia the river measures more than a mile in width; at what was once a famous landmark, McCalls Ferry, it has narrowed to a quarter of a mile. The banks on each side are high and wooded, and one who knows even a little about rivers will speculate about the volume and depth of the current. On the east, Pequea Creek originates in level farmlands, then like its smaller southern neighbor the Tucquan, plunges through a steep and rocky glen to add more volume to the river. The Pequea as it sings along could tell a fascinating story of German-speaking "plain people" from Switzerland, the displaced persons of their day who settled along the streams of Lancaster County.

Making their way down the Rhine, groups of Mennonites were assisted by fellow-believers in Holland. From there in 1709 eight families sailed to England and thence after a long delay to Philadelphia. Tossed by storms, attacked by pirates, they reached port in six months. Assured of land, they tramped on an Indian trail through the primeval forest until they reached Pequea Creek and the peace that was the hope of their souls. So overjoyed were they that they sent one of their number back to Switzerland to bid their fellow-believers follow.

The dwelling of their leader stands today; some of their descendants own the property assigned them in 1700 by the colonial government. Benjamin Rush declared that "a German farm may be distinguished from the farms of other citizens of the State, by the superior size of their barns, the plain but compact form of their houses, the height of their enclosures, the extent of their orchards, the fertility of their fields, the luxuriance of their meadows, and a general appearance of plenty and neatness in everything that belongs to them." To this day Rush's description is accurate in the Pennsylvania-German areas along the Susquehanna and the streams large and small that flow into it. The stone or brick houses are built to shelter generation after generation. Rotation of crops, the use of animal rather than commercial fertilizers, the accumulated farming skill of successive generations have combined to enrich the fields planted with corn and wheat and tobacco.

Not all the Mennonites remained on the Pequea Creek; hundreds migrated to

Photo: J. Horace McFarland Co.
The Wake Robin (*Trillium grandiflorum*) clothes some hillsides of the river.

the West and even to Canada. This largest group of the so-called "sect people" has helped to build the nation. Some, like General Eisenhower, for the sake of the country that received them, have cultivated the fields of war.

To the north of the Pequea, Cocalico Creek flows into Conestoga Creek and on into the Susquehanna. Here a strange yet able fanatic, Conrad Beissel, founded Ephrata, a community of German Baptists. At the height of its success it had a membership of three hundred, some living as celibates in the towering medieval buildings, their walls constructed of mud and straw, which Beissel erected, others in normal family relations on nearby farms.

HARRISBURG TO THE MARYLAND BORDER

Cultivating the rich soil, running five mills and a printing press, the community was certain to prosper. The women prepared food, spun and wove the rough material for the white robes, like the robes of Capuchins, worn by all, and illuminated Bible passages with delicate skill to ornament the walls. Here Peter Miller, a scholar, translated the Declaration of Independence into seven languages; here also he translated the famous Martyr Book of the Mennonites from its original Dutch into German, so that it could be comprehended by the German pilgrims to Pennsylvania. During the Revolution they saw many of the unbound pages carried away to serve as wadding for guns.

Surely neither the main stream of the Susquehanna nor any of its tributaries witnessed a stranger sight than the monks and nuns marching in solemn procession to their low-ceiled chapel at midnight, nor heard stranger sounds than the ethereal compositions in seven parts, sung through half-closed lips.

Convinced that the brethren and sisters were becoming too proud of their

Photo: J. Horace McFarland Co.
On hillsides and islands are found masses of native ferns.

From Shenk's Ferry, on the pool above the Holtwood Dam, the wooded hills crowd closer to the narrowing river.

Photo: R. B. McFarland

possessions, Beissel burned down one building. Nevertheless, his followers continued to admire and obey him. Exalted by their praise, he assumed both the good and evil prerogatives of royalty, and eventually became a victim of bad habits.

Today only two buildings remain, set in grassy lawns above the Cocalico. Close by in the little community cemetery lie Beissel and Miller and others who called themselves "the solitary," and on the hillside lie possibly two hundred American soldiers of the five hundred cared for in the cloister after the Battle of Brandywine. The State, at last convinced that here is a precious and rare survival of German medieval architecture, soon to be abandoned in the Pennsylvania towns and villages, is now beginning the long process of restoration.

The "sect people" formed but a small proportion of the immense migration of Germans, who belonged chiefly to the established Lutheran and Reformed churches. The firm continuance of the Mennonites, Amish Mennonites and Dunkers in the faith of their fathers, their unchanged way of life and their practically unmodified style of dress continue to distinguish them. The *wanderlust*, which is as characteristic as their love of home, has carried them across the continent so that their plain garb is seen wherever there is good land, but it is along the Susquehanna and its tributaries that they seem especially to belong.

The Octoraro flows into Maryland before it enters the Susquehanna. On its upper course in Lancaster County at Christiana, Negroes gathered to prevent the return of one of their number to slavery, and the resulting bloodshed was one of the events that brought on the Civil War.

The city of Lancaster, with its spreading suburbs, its encircling villages, its large and prosperous industries that have a pleasant rural quality, its schools, its beautiful churches, substantial meeting houses and famous markets, lies in the embrace of Conestoga Creek. Like the Codorus, the Conestoga filled a canal and thus became part of the long waterway that accompanied the Susquehanna.

On the west bank of the Susquehanna, approached by roads through the forest, stands the Indian Steps Museum in which there are thousands of Indian artifacts gathered by John E. Vandersloot. The museum is under the care of the Conservation Society of York County and the Pennsylvania Water & Power Company, whose Holtwood Dam, built in 1910, covers the rocky steps carved out by the Indians. The soil in low places is black with fine coal washed from the

At McCalls Ferry, just above the present Holtwood Dam, is the narrowest point of the Susquehanna between Sunbury and the Chesapeake. Here, in 1815, Theodore Burr, famous bridge builder of his day, erected his engineering masterpiece: a two-span bridge across the gorge, the longer span having a length of three hundred and sixty feet, framed entirely of wood timbers. Unfortunately, the bridge was short-lived, being destroyed by an ice gorge and flood in March, 1818. From old records a painting of the bridge, here reproduced, was made for the Pennsylvania Water & Power Company.

Photo: *Courtesy Pennsylvania Water & Power Co.*

HARRISBURG TO THE MARYLAND BORDER

mines a hundred miles upstream. Dredged from the river bed, especially from the dam and converted into steam, it supplies additional power in periods of drought.

Deep under the dam lies the road of which McCalls Ferry was once a part. Here the river was spanned by one of Burr's four great Susquehanna covered bridges. Of them all it was most daring in construction, most romantic in situation and most tragic in its fate. The crossing was important because it shortened the distance from Lancaster to Baltimore and thence to Washington by ten miles. Also, the ferry was frequently unsafe because of the swiftness of the deep current and the piling up of ice.

Burr not only planned the structure to its last detail but supervised its building. He also left a vivid and little-known account of its construction, of the river in flood and of the courage and hardihood of his workmen. There are many descriptions of the beauty of the river but few of its might. For that reason Burr's report is included here.

He wrote from Harrisburg on February 26, 1815, to his partner, Reuben Field, in Waterford, New York. His letter was printed in *Niles Weekly Register* on November 15, 1815, and reprinted in the Papers of the Lancaster County Historical Society, Volume XI, Number 4, in April, 1907. Gratitude is due each of its preservers.

Photo: LaRue Lemer

The "Camelback" Bridge was erected by Theodore Burr at Harrisburg in 1817. The east section, shown here, was destroyed and rebuilt several times.

Photo: O. P. Beckley
The west section of the "Camelback" Bridge at Harrisburg was the longest-lived of the Burr bridges, being removed, not destroyed, in 1902, after the east section was carried away by flood and ice.

He had revived in his bridges the use of the Palladian truss, an arch which, resting on piers, supported the weight of the floor, the beams and the roof. At McCalls Ferry he had succeeded at the time of his writing in raising the long arch at the west side of the river, which he describes, and had returned to his home in Harrisburg. His joy was that of a man who has achieved an almost impossible task and wishes to share his satisfaction with a friend who understands the problems he has solved and the perils he has overcome.

"This arch is, without doubt, the greatest in the world. Its length between the abutment and pier, is three hundred and sixty feet, four inches, its chord line three hundred and sixty-seven feet. The width of the main part of the bridge is thirty-two feet; the wings of the pier spread eleven feet eight inches on each side, which makes a base of fifty-five feet, four inches. At the abutment, the wings spread seventeen feet each, which makes a base of sixty-six feet. The altitude or rise of the arch is thirty-one feet. The arch is double, and the two segments are combined by king-posts seven feet in length between the shoulders and are united to the arch by lock-work. Between the king-posts are truss braces and counteracting braces. The arch stands firm and remarkably easy, without the least struggling in any part of the work.

"It will be difficult to convey to you the process by which we finally succeeded in surmounting the almost unconquerable difficulties opposed to its erection, not only by nature, but by all the elements combined.

"In the first place we raised it on floats lying in the water, ranged along the

Photo: Courtesy Miss Marian Cook

A sailboat at York Y. M. C. A. Camp Minqua on the pool of the Holtwood Dam.

Photo: Courtesy Miss Marian Cook

Camp Minqua, run by the York Y. M. C. A., is one of many such recreation places that take advantage of the slack water behind Holtwood Dam.

shore nearly a quarter of a mile below the abutment. The floats were placed at proper distances, with their ends to the shore, and on each of them were raised two bents or frames, varying in height to correspond with the curve of the arch. This made sixteen bents, on which the grand and enormous structure was raised, amidst tremendous storms and tempests accompanied with floods and whirls and the bursting of waters. The scene at times was truly terrific. Frequently, in the darkest nights we were under the necessity of going between the floats, and from one to the other, on small timbers, over a depth of one hundred feet of water, in order either to shorten or lengthen the ropes by which they were fastened, and to brace off or haul out in the floats, as the water rose or fell . . . You must understand that storm and wind are much more frequent and tremendous at this place, than at any other."

The surface of the water was never steady but rose and fell daily ten to twelve feet, in addition to the tremendous rise in time of freshets.

HARRISBURG TO THE MARYLAND BORDER

"The arch stood length-ways up and down the river, along the shore of uneven points and projections of rocks, which kept us always in jeopardy, in consequence of the rising and falling of the water. On the 17th of December, 1814, we had the whole in readiness to move up to the abutment, and on the same day the anchor-ice began to run a little. The next, which was the day we had fixed upon to move the arch to its place, the ice ran in still greater quantities, and about one o'clock it stopped for the space of about half a mile, and began to crowd the floats. It continued to move for more than one hundred miles above where the river is from one and a-half to two miles wide; whereas, at this place you will observe it is only six hundred and nine feet in high water and in low water the whole river runs in the space of three hundred and forty-eight feet."

Under the pressure of ice the floats not only moved up and down but were carried twenty or thirty feet downstream. Fortunately, though they were crushed,

The water front at Camp Minqua.

Photo: Courtesy Miss Marian Cook

arch and scaffolding remained undamaged. Braces burst and the immense structure careened toward the shore but still no permanent damage was done.

It was now time to transfer the arch built in two sections from the floats to the frozen river and to move it to the abutment and piers that had been prepared.

"I had 18 men employed at that business and I presume that on an average they were in, up to their arms, forty times each in one day. The ice here is made up of floating ice from one-fourth inch to two inches thick. It forms from fifty to two hundred and fifty miles above the bridge, where the water is not very rapid, but very wide; and in some winters runs constantly for three or four weeks without stopping. From the head of Turkeyville falls to within three-fourths of a mile of the bridge, a distance of about fifteen miles, there is almost one continued fall, the bed of the river abounding with rocks that break the ice very fine. The river being so long and wide above, there is an immense quantity of this ice formed, and so very narrow at the bridge, that there it becomes an immense mass from twelve to fifteen feet deep, before it stops. When this takes place, all the ice from above drives beneath into the deep water, until it becomes from sixty to eighty feet deep; and you may, by digging down three feet take a pole sixty feet long, and with the strength of your hands run it down the whole length, and find no termination of what is called the mush ice."

The soft ice had to be bridged so that it would hold the great weight of arch and scaffold. Snow and rain added new hardships. Nevertheless, little by little the arch was moved upstream and elevated to the abutment on which it was to rest. Then the other half was moved and elevated to the pier nearest the shore. The whole process of moving consumed about three weeks.

On January 30, 1815, at nine o'clock at night, the whole arch "was brought to its peaceful height and curve and then united in the center." The next day every part was examined and the scaffolding knocked away. When darkness came, the workers continued by the light of huge fires at each end of the bridge.

Not only were the skill of the engineering and the effort involved extraordinary, but so was the community effort.

"During the whole of this struggle, the humane feelings and kind dispositions of the inhabitants, for twelve to fourteen miles distance on both sides of the river were manifested to a degree that I believe was scarcely ever equalled. They vol-

Photo: R. B. McFarland

Pequea, on the Lancaster County shore, is mostly a summer colony of people who make good use of the lake created by the dam below.

The Tucquan Club House on the York County shore was once a warehouse on the Susquehanna and Tidewater Canal. From the clubhouse lawn is seen the lake-like pool above Holtwood.

Photo: R. B. McFarland

untarily assisted from day to day; so that from the 8th of January to the first of February, I had of this class from forty to one hundred and twenty men every day. They came early, stayed till dark, and returned home after night . . . One day we would call on Lancaster county, the next on York, and sometimes on both in the same day. To move an arch of such an enormous weight, fifty and sixty feet in the air, was no small business; and, had it not been for the friendship of these people, I almost doubt whether I should ever have effected the object."

Surely the river never saw a stranger sight! None of the other great bridges had a setting of ice and darkness and wind and storm in a narrow space, or such depth of water beneath. Even so there was but one person injured and he, having fallen fifty-four feet and hit twice on the braces, landed in the water and was at work after two days.

There remains no contemporary picture of the bridge. One of the few facts recorded about it is that Thaddeus Stevens rode across, on his way from Bel Air, Maryland, to Lancaster, before it was quite completed, and almost lost his life. Various reasons are given for his journey. It is the author's speculation that having been familiar with small Burr bridges in Vermont, he went to see the Palladian or "Burr" truss.

A few newspapers of the time reported the fate of the bridge. From Sunbury, on March 5, 1818, reports of rain began. "The rain fell with a great violence and little intermission the whole of Sunday night and part of the next day. The water had risen to unusual heights." Meager items followed slowly in what newspapers there were. Said the Philadelphia *Gazette* on March 10: "We are sorry to hear that the elegant bridge at McCalls Ferry has been carried away. The flood and multiplicity of ice, has not been known to have been so great for many years. We deem it a public loss."

A public loss it was. Of its destruction we know only the fact. Did it happen by day or night? Were fires built on the high bank so that masons and carpenters might watch in awe the last end of their weary and devoted toil? Was there loud grinding and crashing, or did the sound of rain and wind dull the splitting of the timbers? Did morning lighten a scene of ruin or was all gone, swept clear, the sun dancing on the waters? Did the floods carry it, roof and walls, arches and stays, in huge connected masses downstream, astonishing the fishing villages as it passed,

Just above the breast of Holtwood Dam, the hills narrow toward the gorge at McCalls Ferry. Before the building of the dam, this was a dreaded section of the river for boatmen.

Photo: R. B. McFarland

HARRISBURG TO THE MARYLAND BORDER

or did it long lie broken on the rocks on the lower river? What did Burr think or say when the news of the catastrophe reached him?

Today the area is called Holtwood, and here a dam spanned the river before Safe Harbor was constructed. Each dam is part of the others; since the same river fills and the same power companies control them, the importance of their interdependence is understood. On the eastern slope of the gorge steep roads connect the offices and the houses of employees in the village of Holtwood. On the opposite side the old road, descending more gradually though still steeply, through a glen dark with rhododendron, leads now into the deep dam. The Pennsylvania Water & Power Company, unwilling that all remembrance of Burr's bridge should perish, has put on canvas a representation of what it must have been. Except that under the roof heavy lattice has been substituted for the trusses, one so enormous, the picture is doubtless accurate. No wonder that men marveled and went out of their way to see the great structure! How happy on a wild night in "the whirl of wind and water" must men and horses have been to draw their loaded wagons in under the protecting roof!

When Burr died, he was still building bridges, but it is likely that public opinion realized that the current at McCalls Ferry, speeding as through a flume, was too powerful for human strength and ingenuity to oppose. Three and a half years later he succumbed; where we know, but not how. A half century and another builder, John Roebling, twisted steel wires into cables to hang bridges over the Ohio and the Niagara and the East River. Another half century and at Northumberland, Harrisburg and Columbia, where Burr had built his wooden bridges, concrete reinforced with steel carried the weight of trains across the Susquehanna. Only at McCalls Ferry, since Burr is gone, is there no bridge. Quietly between the steep hills lies the dam; steely blue, like the water in shadow, rise the pyramids of coal; overhead may wheel an eagle, companioning perhaps one of his own kind instead of the many that must have scanned wonderingly from on high the strange ways of men in the days of the great hooded arch.

Charles Weathers Bump shared Burr's awe of and admiration for the lower river. "Shut in as it is by high, steep ridges, this portion of the river, the last before its waters are spread out into the broad Chesapeake bay, has been very appropriately called the Highlands of the Susquehanna.

PENNSYLVANIA'S SUSQUEHANNA

"One rocky spur after another juts out into the river and forms a series of bold, natural abutments upon both sides. At the base of these high bluffs a railroad creeps along on the east bank and the Tidewater canal has been cut on the west bank, both of them often so near the river that it seems as if train or boat would fall over into the water or else jam its nose into some titanic wall of granite or slate. Along the hillsides between the jagged rocks are wild growths, a number of creeks, and streams and frequent deep ravines. Sometimes there are homes, but the

Photo: J. Horace McFarland

In midsummer the Bergamot (*Monarda fistulosa*) may be found among the hills.

HARRISBURG TO THE MARYLAND BORDER

Photo: O. P. Beckley
A late summer and early fall native flower, the New England Aster (*A. novæ-angliæ*) is abundant in the Susquehanna valley.

ridges are too rugged to permit of much cultivation and so the hills have been left practically undisturbed, save where rocks were blasted to make way for canal or railroad.

"Between the hills is the river, so narrow at some places that one is tempted to try and throw a stone across, and again spread out so as to make room for rocky islets, ponderous, grim-looking bowlders and occasionally an island large enough to afford a chance for trees or tall grass. At least a dozen times some distinctly

Approaching the Holtwood Dam from the south, the observer notes the rugged character of the region. The rocks below the breast of the dam are indicative of the wildness of the Susquehanna at this point before being tamed for "white coal."

Photo: R. B. McFarland

HARRISBURG TO THE MARYLAND BORDER

marked ledge of rocks extends from bank to bank, and over these the river pitches into rapids, swirling, tossing and foaming, with a strength which surprises one, but which shows what dangers the lumbermen and boatmen met when they formerly descended the river. The drouth this summer (1899) has made the keen edges of the rocks even more apparent, and so has added to the dread which they inspire.

"The great bowlders in midstream rise up in such grotesque and unnatural shapes that we instinctively feel that some tremendous force grimly fashioned them in the primeval ages. They and the stony ridges which cast their shadows across the river are never-failing sources of interest to the geologist. They must have been among the earliest of the world's creations and are so hard that an ordinary hammer can do nothing with them.

"Nature's climax is in the seven miles between Safe Harbor and McCall's Ferry. There the hills are steepest, the river wildest, the bowlders and rocky islets most abundant. McCall's Ferry is the point watched with greatest apprehension in the spring by the people of Port Deposit. It is twenty-one miles above Port Deposit and eighteen below Columbia. At that point the river forms a gorge so narrow that if the ice jams in its descent there is almost sure to be a disastrous flood when it breaks again."

Here the river has taken toll of many lives. In late March, 1949, two employees at the Holtwood plant, lured by the spring weather, celebrated a holiday by fishing from an island. All went well until as they rowed toward the west shore, a rising wind suddenly capsized their boat. A brakeman on a Pennsylvania Railroad train moving slowly along the bank saw their desperate situation and halted his train at the nearest tower. From there he notified Baltimore headquarters, and the urgent message was relayed by short wave to Holtwood. One of the two men was saved; the other was carried downstream.

Maryland lies about ten miles below Holtwood, and in this distance no highways accompany the river and few roads approach from east or west. To the west lie towns and villages with revealing names: Castle Fin, Bangor and on the very border, Cardiff. The nature of the rock bordering the river may be guessed; here on both banks are partly abandoned but once productive slate quarries operated by Welshmen who imported the names of Welsh towns. As there are two Conewago creeks, one on each side of the river, so there are two sections called Peach Bottom, originally Beach Bottom.

Above Peach Bottom the river has begun not to widen—there is no space to widen—but to deepen. To the south lies Conowingo Dam, which is at the same time a bridge across which one may drive and look back upon Pennsylvania's Susquehanna, not yet Maryland's, or downstream upon the stalking transmission towers. Here is the last fall of the river and here is garnered all its great power.

If you are so fortunate as to be invited by Dr. and Mrs. Herbert Beck to accompany them, a day's excursion on the lower river will enrich a year's memory. It is impossible to be equipped with sufficient historical, geological, botanical or ornithological information to understand all that you see. If you approach through Lancaster County and Drumore Township, by way of the birthplace of Robert Fulton or the seven-fold spring, they alone will give you food for long reflection. Seeing them, however, only begins or closes the day.

From Cutler's Point spreads a magnificent landscape. The powerful current, still dropping swiftly toward the bay, speeds between islands cut by potholes, some opening to the rapidly moving water, some not yet wholly pierced and containing stones, perhaps strong trap-rock from York Haven, in the unfinished depressions. The rocks, too, are hard; the holes have been a long time in the making, and it may be years before there comes a flood sufficiently strong to whirl them round and round. The day will come, however, when they too will slip into the river.

If your excursion is in May, your eye may follow incredulously from Cutler's Point a line of heavenly blue. This is the bloom of *Paulownia tomentosa*, the seed of which has been blown from an old tree beside a farmhouse on the hill. Thus does Japan deck the Susquehanna. Thus also Russia, since the tree, a native of Japan, was named for Anna Paulowna, daughter of Czar Paul I.

Along the river at the mouth of western-flowing Fishing Creek, one of many Susquehanna tributaries of the same name, you will find the owner of a powerful motorboat, familiar with all the passageways between the islands. He will carry you first downstream to Mount Johnson Island, engulfed all but its summit in Conowingo Dam. Here rare plants like the prickly pear cactus, their seeds waterborne, flourish far from their native habitat. From the mainland, the island, thickly set with tall trees, recalls Böcklin's grim picture, "The Isle of the Dead."

Photo: R. B. McFarland

Mount Johnson Island, one of the few islands of any elevation in the Susquehanna, is a sanctuary for the Bald Eagle, emblematic bird of American freedom. On a calm day it is reflected picturesquely in the slack water of Conowingo Dam.

Peach Bottom, Lancaster County, is about the last settlement accessible by road before coming to the Mason and Dixon Line. It was the eastern terminus of the "farthest south" Pennsylvania ferry on the Susquehanna.

Here also for many years a pair of eagles nested in a tall tree, theirs the only protected eagle-aerie in the world. As you encircle the island you can see the black scraggly nest, not a comfortable home when viewed from beneath, but the birthplace and shelter of many families.

Each year the mother visited newly cut hayfields to claw at the swaths, doubtless seeking a young rabbit for her eaglets. Her absence from the nest in 1948 caused ornithologists to fear that she was permanently gone, possibly a victim of the gun of some farmer who believed old fables about the carrying off of lambs or young children. In 1949, to the joy of those who watch the skies, the nest was again occupied.

Your navigator will bring you to port, not without considerable slowing against the force of the current, on an island in midstream. If you are like the writer of this text, amazed and enchanted, you will let others unpack the lunch and set

HARRISBURG TO THE MARYLAND BORDER

the picnic table and you will wander, your eye now marking a handsome holly tree, now peering down through a circular opening at the river flowing briskly beneath, perhaps making strange sounds.

Your thoughts will range far north. There is the loop of the North Branch as it enters from New York State, returns and enters again. You think of the immense pine forest, slanting northeast from Bedford County, its greatest and grandest growth on the Susquehanna's West Branch. You remember that some of its timbers bound into rafts rode the flood past this spot where you sit. You recall that tall masts into which they were spliced stood firm against the winds over all the seas of the world. In reality, a tall clipper should be one of the illustrations of this book.

You hear a mournful reverberation. Is it the bell of the Moravian Indians carried far, far away from its belfry at Wyalusing? You hear the crack of the

Photo: R. B. McFarland

Peach Bottom, York County, was the western end of the ferry that here crossed the river. The pool of the Conowingo Dam can be very rough when whipped by strong winds.

From Cutler's Point on the east bank of the Susquehanna, there is a charming view of the river, here like a lake, and its surrounding hills. Mount Johnson Island rises to the left and the distant hills are beyond the Pennsylvania–Maryland line. On a quiet day, the water

woodsman's axe, the shrill mine whistle giving notice that coal is rising in the shaft. Children laugh on beaches, skates ring, and singing echoes over the water.

There is Harrisburg, its dome agleam in the setting sun, its lovely islands appearing to float on the wide river. There lengthen the miles of furnaces and stockpiles. There lie the broad dams, now quiet, now loudly roaring.

Is the river useless? It transported millions of feet of timber and thousands of tons of coal. The canal, filled by its waters, transported travelers and the grain from a thousand fields. Has it no power? It lights cities and moves long trains. Is it too broad and too shallow? See it at McCalls Ferry. Is it too narrow? Look down from the bluff at Wrightsville. Has it no history? For it races have contended, and beside it the dispossessed of many nations have found hope and prosperity. It has provided highways for millions, not on its surface, but by its side.

Photo: R. B. McFarland

reflects the sky and the surrounding hills, whether the soft green of early spring, the mature green of midsummer or the bright tree colors of autumn. In the whole Susquehanna valley it would be difficult to find a more beautiful outlook.

The cities on its banks are not wholly lovely. But there are miles of the river and its swift tributaries where one may meet only a deer in a long walk—or perhaps a bear. The white-headed eagle will long soar if we will effectively protect him; the golden eagle is not unknown. The halcyon, which we call the kingfisher, still dives and emerges, his dripping dinner in his beak. The light of evening is no less lovely, its reflection no less rosy. The river's lovers may still, as did Lloyd Mifflin,

> "Lie here along the reedy shore
> Where Susquehanna spreads her liquid miles,
> To watch the circles from the dripping oar,
> To see the halcyon dip, the eagle soar;
> To drift at dusk around these Indian isles,
> Or dream at noon beneath the sycamore."

INDEX

Accomac, 188
Accomac Creek, 189
Adams County, 187
Albany Treaty, 127
Alfarata, 93
Aliquippa Gap, 92
Allegheny Mountains, 75, 93, 97, 101, 166, 173, 177, 191
Allegheny Plateau, 99, 165
Allegheny ridges, 149
Allegheny River, 60, 150
Allen, Richard S., 154
Allenwood, 91
American Car and Foundry Company, 51
Amish, 109, 110
Amity Hall, 113, 166, 170
Andaste Indians, 3, 14
Anderson's Ferry, 189
Antes Fort, 74
Aqueduct, 165
Arbutus, trailing (illustrated), 129
Ardenheim, 101, 107
Ashley, Dr. George, 6, 8
Asylum, 24, 26, 33, 37
Athens, 9, 13, 14, 18, 20, 30, 118, 167
Athens Academy, 13, 167
Aughwick Creek, 109
Avondale, 44

Bainbridge, 170, 186
Bald Eagle, Chief, 102
Bald Eagle Creek, 63, 77, 79, 87, 102
Bald Eagle Mountain, 70, 80
Bald Eagle Ridge, 89
Baltimore, 71, 103, 127, 171, 176, 179, 181, 193, 209, 223
Bangor, 223
Barré, Isaac, 51
Barree, 105
Bartlett, William H., 8
Bartram, John, 27, 66, 121
Beach Bottom, 224
Beck, Dr. and Mrs. Herbert, 9, 224
Beck, Dr. Herbert H., 182
Bedford, 93, 95, 97, 153
Bedford County, 5, 66, 93, 101, 227
Beechwood, 105
Beissel, Conrad, 204, 207
Bel Air, Md., 217
Bellefonte, 163
Bennet, Katherine, 9
Bergamot (illustrated), 220

Bergstresser, Nellie Rupley, 9
Berks County, 17
Berry Mountain, 130, 133, 154
Berwick, 51
Bethlehem, 29
Bethlehem Steel Company, 175, 178, 180
Billmeyer, 188
Binghamton, N. Y., 171
Blacklog Mountain, 109, 170
Bloomsburg, 51
Blue Hill, 91, 114, 118, 122, 125
Blue Mountain, 109
Blue Mountains, 177
Blue Ridge Mountains, xiv, 110, 152, 174
Boston, 71, 135
Bowen, Dr. and Mrs. Earl, 9
Braddock, General, 27, 95
Bradford County, 1, 13, 16, 23, 47, 193
Brady, Captain John, 59
Brainerd, David, 142
Brandywine, Battle of, 207
Brulé, Etienne, 14, 17, 34, 37, 59, 121
Brush, Frederic, 53, 93, 175
Brush Mountain, 101
Bryant, William Cullen, 8, 145
Bucknell University, 90, 91
Buffalo Creek, 91
Buffalo Mountain, 133
Buffalo, N. Y., 165
Bull, Ole, 81, 87
Bump, Charles Weathers, 181, 196, 219
Burr, Aaron, 97
Burr, Theodore, 118, 154, 157, 177, 189, 208, 209, 210, 217, 219
Butler, Captain Zebulon, 27
Butler, Colonel John, 27

Calhoun, John C., 97
California, 109
Cambria County, 53, 61
Cambridge, 57
Camelback Bridge, 209, 210
Cameron County, 76
Cameron, Donald, 157
Cameron, James, 157
Cameron, Simon, 157
Campbell's Ledge, 26, 40
Camp Minqua, 211, 212, 213
Canada, 62, 151, 204
Cape of Good Hope, 71
Capuchins, 205
Carantouan, 14

INDEX

Carbon County, 41
Carbondale, 40, 41
Cardiff, 223
Carlisle, 145, 150, 151
Carthaginians, 201
Castle Fin, 223
Catawissa Creek, 3, 51
Cave Mountain, 101
Cayuga Indians, 19
Center County, 63
Central Oak Heights, 88
Chambersburg, 99, 110
Chamber's Ferry, 154
Champlain, 14, 17
Chemung River, 13, 16, 20, 154, 191
Cherry Tree, 52, 60
Chesapeake Bay, 17, 53, 60, 71, 73, 79, 208, 219
Chest Creek, 61
Chickies Rock, 170, 189, 190, 191, 192
Chinklacamoose, 61
Christiana, 207
Church, Jerry, 62, 87
Church of the Brethren, 107
Clark's Ferry, x, 112, 136, 138, 145, 147, 166, 170
Clay, Henry, 97
Clearfield, 58, 61, 76, 77
Clearfield County, 53, 60, 76
Clearfield Creek, 61
Clemson's Ferry, 154
Clinton County, 62, 63, 76, 79
Clinton, General George, 29, 69
Cly, 184
Cocalico Creek, 107, 204, 207
Cocolamus Creek, 111
Codorus Creek, 187, 207
Coleridge, Samuel Taylor, 115
Columbia, 75, 118, 131, 154, 166, 170, 172, 173, 181, 189, 193, 194, 195, 196, 201, 203, 219, 223
Columbia–Wrightsville Bridge, 191
Conejohela, 5, 6, 9, 194, 196, 199
Conemaugh River, 75
Conestoga Creek, 3, 197, 204, 207
Conestoga Indians, 3
Conestoga wagons, 145
Conewago Creek, 3, 187
Conewago Falls, 171, 183, 185, 186
Connecticut, 27, 37, 41, 51, 154, 195
Conococheague Creek, 145
Conodoguinet Creek, 3, 101, 145, 147, 191, 199, 201
Conowingo Bridge, 9
Conowingo Dam, 1, 6, 203, 224, 225, 228
Conservation Society of York County, 207
Cornwallis, General, 33
Cove Mountain, x, 140, 144, 146, 150

Covenhoven, Robert, 59
Cresap, Thomas, 195
Cumberland County, xiv, 159, 202
Cumberland Valley, 150
Curtin, Governor Andrew, 111
Curwensville, 56
Cutler's Point, 224, 228

Dalmatia, 124, 126
Danville, 49, 50, 51, 171
Dauphin, 143, 171
Dauphin County, 137, 150, 174
Dauphin Narrows, x, 144
Declaration of Independence, 205
Delaware and Lackawanna Railroad, 39
Delaware Bay, 71
Delaware Indians, 19, 21, 27, 36, 97
Delaware River, 9, 14, 154
de Noailles, Louis, 33
Dewart, 81
Dickens, Charles, 157, 168, 170, 179
Dogwood (illustrated), 7
Driftwood, 83
Drumore Township, 186, 224
Duncan Island, 113, 142
Duncannon, 6, 75, 93, 103, 118, 140, 142, 145, 163
Dunkelberger, Dr. G. F., 9
Dunning Creek, 97, 101, 191
Durell Creek, 33
Durell, Stephen, 33

Eagle County, 63
Eagles Mere, 82, 89
East Bloomsburg, 48
Easton, 29
East River, 219
Eaton, Alice R., 1, 9
Edison, Thomas, 125
Edmonds, Walter D., 168
Egle, Dr. William H., 154
Eisenhower, General Dwight D., 204
Elder (illustrated), 91
Elk Lake, 13
Elm (illustrated), 31
Endless Mountains, 22
England, 33
Enola, 6, 147
Ephrata, 204
Ephrata Cloister, 107
Erie Canal, 165, 167, 168
Erie Railroad, 10, 11, 12
Ettwein, Bishop, 36
Evans, Lewis, 25, 27, 121
Everett, 101, 107
Evitt Mountain, 101

231

Falls, 35, 39
Falmouth, 170
Faris, Dr. John T., 153, 193
Fellenbaum, Edith, 9
Ferns (illustrated), 205
Fiddle Lake, 13
Field, Reuben, 209
Fisher Ridge, 124, 126, 128, 137
Fishing Creek, 51, 224
Forest Lake, 13
Forster's Island, 154, 156, 160
Fort Augusta, 122
Fort Halifax, 154
Fort Niagara, 29
Forty Fort, 27, 51
Foster, Stephen, 13, 167
Foster, William B., Jr., 167
France, 115
Franklin and Marshall College, 182, 199
Franklin, Benjamin, 95
Franklin County, 145
Frankstown Branch, 105
Freeburg, 135
Friedenshütten, 36
Fryling, Charles A., 170, 172
Fulton, Robert, 165, 224

Gettysburg, 110, 189
Gilbert, Dr. Russell W., 109
Girty, Simon, 141
Glaze, Mrs. Olive Aucher, 133, 135
Gooch, Governor, 22
Granville, 104
Gray's Ferry, 11
Great Bend, 10, 11, 13, 15
Great Valley, 174
Grove, Peter, 55
Grove Run, 57
Gulf of Mexico, 53

Haldeman Island, 142, 181
Halifax, 141, 143
Hanickhungo Indians, 19
Harrisburg, x, xiv, 5, 6, 21, 63, 71, 75, 81, 101, 110, 118, 122, 127, 131, 147, 149, 152, 153, 154, 155, 156, 157, 158, 160, 162, 164, 166, 167, 168, 170, 174, 176, 177, 178, 179, 180, 189, 209, 210, 219, 228
Harrisburg Kipona, 158, 161
Harris' Ferry, 29, 127, 150, 151, 154
Harris, John, 127, 149, 151, 174, 175
Harris, John, Jr., 174
Harrison State Park, 87
Harrison Wright Falls, 45
Hartley, Colonel Thomas, 29, 59
Harvey Creek, 51

Harvey Lake, 51
Hemlock (illustrated), 72
Hemlock Creek, 51
Hepatica (illustrated), 4
Herndon, 123, 133
Highlands of the Susquehanna, 219
Highspire, 175, 180
Hill Island, 177, 183
Hogpen Lock, 170
Holland, 203
Hollidaysburg, 101, 102, 163
Holtwood Dam, 1, 5, 6, 9, 186, 206, 207, 208, 211, 212, 216, 218, 219, 222
Hooflander Mountain, 124, 137
Hoopes, Edmund Darlington, 9
Hopewell, 94
Hudson River, 14, 17, 154, 165
Hunter's Gap, 160
Huntingdon, 98, 107, 167, 170
Huntingdon County, 101, 105
Huntingdon, Selina, Countess of, 107
Hyner, 64
Hyner's View, 87

Illinois, 62
Indiana County, 53, 61
Indian Steps Museum, 207
International Correspondence School, 47
Iroquois Long House, 122
Iroquois tribes, 3, 14, 17, 36, 121, 195
Isle of Que, 120, 127, 132

Jack's Mountain, 107, 109
Jack's Narrows, 100, 107
Jemison, Mary, 27
Jersey Shore, 74, 76, 166
Joe-Pye Weed (illustrated), 69
Johnstown, 75, 81
Junction Canal, 167
Juniata Bridge, 112, 113, 136
Juniata Canal, 167
Juniata College, 107
Juniata County, 137

Karthaus, 62
Karthaus, Peter, 62
Keating, 63, 81
Kekkachtanin Hills, 21
Kentucky, 62
Kettle Creek, 81
King of England, 127
Kingston, 51
Kipona, Harrisburg, 158, 161
Kishacoquillas Creek, 106, 109
Kiskiminitas Canal, 166
Kiskiminitas Creek, 101, 165

INDEX

Kitchen Creek, 45, 51
Kittatinny Mountains, 177
Krauth, Harriet B., 9

Laceyville, 31
Lackawanna River, 3, 9, 13, 30, 36, 40, 51
Lafayette, General, 33, 179
Lake Erie, 165
Lake Otsego, 29, 69
Lancaster, 59, 182, 207, 209, 217
Lancaster County, 107, 145, 186, 189, 197, 203, 207, 215, 217, 224, 226
Lancaster County Historical Society, 209
Laurel Lake, 13
Lauxmont Dairy Farm, 196
Leah Lake, 13
Lee, General Robert E., 110, 189
Lehigh River, 9
Lehigh Valley Railroad, 39
Lewisburg, 63, 90, 91
Lewisburg and Northumberland Railroad, 81
Lewistown, 104, 106, 108, 110, 166
Lewistown Narrows, 106, 108
Limestone Creek, 81
Lincoln Highway, 99, 194
Lincoln, President Abraham, 110, 111
Little Juniata, 101, 105
Little Norway, 132
Little Tuscarora Creek, 132
Liverpool, 5, 6, 75, 132, 135, 139, 170
Lochartzburgh, 30, 31
Lock Haven, 63, 65, 67, 70, 71, 73, 77, 79, 87, 102, 118, 166
Logan, John, 109
Long House, 29, 196
Long Level, 5, 194, 196, 198
Lost and Found Creek, 101
Lost Creek, 87
Loyalsock Creek, 80, 89
Lushbaugh, 83, 191
Luzerne County, 38
Lycoming County, 63, 76, 78
Lycoming Creek, 3, 89
Lykens Valley, 139
Lyso, 87
Lytle's Ferry, 154

MacFarland, James, 8
Maclay's Ferry, 15
Mahaffey, 55
Mahanoy Creek, 127
Mahanoy Mountain, 133
Mahantango Creek, 3, 127, 137, 139
Mahantango Mountain, 113, 128, 133, 139
Maine, 83
Mapleton, 107

Marietta, 8, 29, 75, 187, 190, 199
Marsh Run, 180
Marsh Run Army Depot, 178
Martin's Hill Mountain, 101
Martyr Book, 205
Maryland, 4, 18, 99, 163, 171, 193, 195, 201, 207, 223
Marysville, 150
Mason and Dixon Line, 226
Mattawanna, 104
McAlevys Fort, 107
McCalls Ferry, 5, 118, 154, 177, 203, 208, 209, 210, 217, 218, 219, 223, 228
McClellan, Samuel, 132
McClintock, Gilbert S., 9
McFarland, Dr. J. Horace, 9, 89, 160, 170
McFarland, Robert B., 89
McGees Landing, 81
McGees Mills, 54, 61
McKean County, 81
McKees Half Falls, 137
McMaster, John Bach, 75
McMillan, Margaret, 9
McVeytown, 103
Meade, General, 111
Mechanicsburg, 201
Mehoopany Creek, 3, 30
Mertensia (illustrated), 8
Meshoppen Creek, 3, 13, 39
Meynell, Alice, 4
Middleburg, 137
Middle Creek, 132
Middleswarth State Park, 69
Middletown, 29, 177, 178, 182, 183
Mifflin County, 106, 107
Mifflin, Lloyd, 181, 229
Mile Hill, 50, 118, 122
Mill Creek, 100
Miller, Peter, 205
Millersburg, 130
Millerstown, 111, 113
Milton, 81, 88, 131, 171
Miner, Charles, 13, 47
Minnesota, 87
Mississippi River, 95, 151
Missouri, 62
Mocanaqua, 43
Mohawk Indians, 17
Monongahela River, 150
Montgomery, 81, 85
Montgomery Ferry, 170
Montour family, 59
Montour, Madam, 22
Montour Mountain, 90
Montour, "Queen" Esther, 29, 51, 59
Montoursville, 80, 82

233

Montrose, 13
Moravians, German, 36
Morris, Robert, 34
Mosquito Creek, 61, 62, 87, 193
Mountain Laurel (illustrated), 2
Mount Avery, 39
Mount Johnson Island, 1, 224, 225, 228
Mt. Union, 104, 107, 109
Muncy, 28, 81, 82, 85
Muncy Creek, 89
Muncy, Fort, 29
Muncy Hills, 85
Murray, Dr. Elsie, 9, 17
Murray, Louise Wells, 9
Myers, Dr. Richmond E., 8

Nanticoke, 27, 40, 51
National Geographic Society, 37
Nescopeck Creek, 3
Nescopeck Falls, 172
New Bergen, 87
New Berlin, 135
New Buffalo, 134
New Cumberland, 176
New England Aster (illustrated), 221
Newport, 113
Newton-Hamilton, 102
New York City, 29, 71, 135, 165, 193
New York State, 4, 11, 13, 14, 17, 118, 163, 165, 177, 227
Niagara Falls, 11
Niagara River, 219
Nicholson, John, 34, 39
Nitschman, Susanna, 27, 40
North Bend, 87
North Branch Canal, 166
North Carolina, 121
North Mountain, 45, 89
Northumberland, 6, 54, 75, 114, 115, 118, 125, 154, 163, 166, 170, 177, 219
Northumberland County, 76, 137
Northumberland County Historical Society, 133, 170, 173
Northwest Territory, 165
Norway, 87

Oakland, 15
Octoraro Creek, 207
Ohio, 36, 97, 109
Ohio River, 150, 151, 219
Oleona, 87
Oneida Indians, 19
Onojutta, 93
Onondaga, 17, 25, 59, 196
Onondaga Indians, 19
Orbisonia, 107

Ossinepachte, 24
Osterhout, 35
Ostuaga, 22
Oswego, 127
Otzinachson, 53
Oxford, N. Y., 154

Packer Island, 118
Palomar, 109
Parnell Knob, 101
Peach Bottom, 181, 224, 226, 228
Pennamite Wars, 27
Penns Creek, 120, 127, 132
Pennsylvania Canal, 162, 168, 196
Pennsylvania Railroad, 103, 104, 108, 110, 147, 148, 173, 197, 223
Pennsylvania Turnpike, 111, 177, 180
Pennsylvania, University of, 107
Pennsylvania Water & Power Company, 200, 201, 207, 208, 219
Penn, William, 17, 27, 36, 107, 165, 201
Pequea Creek, 3, 203, 204, 215
Petersburg, 105
Peters Mountain, x, 112, 113, 133, 136, 142, 143
Philadelphia, 19, 21, 22, 33, 34, 71, 87, 122, 150, 165, 166, 170, 173, 177, 181, 187, 193, 203
Philadelphia and Erie Railroad, 81, 173
Philadelphia *Gazette*, 217
Phlox (illustrated), 147
Phoenician (?) stone, 202
Pine Creek, 6, 87, 191, 193
Pittsburgh, 103, 168, 177
Pittston, 6, 27, 37, 40, 51
Plymouth, 41, 51
Pomeroy, Stephen, 110
Portage Road, 101
Port Deposit, 223
Port Royal, 110, 111
Port Trevorton, 133, 135, 137
Potomac River, 145
Potter County, 4, 81
Pottsville, 137
Priestley, Joseph, 115, 117, 125

Quaker Lake, 13
Queen Anne, 17
Queen Esther's Town, 29, 30
Queen Marie Antoinette, 26, 33

Ray's Hill, 101
Raystown Branch, 94, 95, 107
Raystown Creek, 93, 97, 101
Reading, 59, 137
Reading Railroad, 81

INDEX

Reed, Thomas Buchanan, 115
Renovo, 67, 76
Rhine River, 203
Rhododendron (illustrated), 4
Richter, Conrad, 97
Ricketts Glen State Park, 45
Riverside, 49
Roberts Lake, 107
Rockville, 170
Rockville Bridge, 148, 149, 151, 152, 170
Rocky Mountains, 75
Roebling, John, 219
Rome, N. Y., 165
Roosevelt, Theodore, 94
Royalton, 182, 183
Rummerfield, 26, 34
Rummerfield, Anthony, 33
Rummerfield Creek, 33
Rush, Benjamin, 203

Safe Harbor Dam, 1, 6, 9, 196, 197, 198, 200, 201, 219, 223
Saguchsanyunt Indians, 19
Santayana, George, 6
Sawuntga Indians, 19
Saxton, 95
Sayre, 14, 16
Schnure, William A., 170
Schoch, Agnes Selin, 9
Schoharie Creek, 17
Schuylkill County, 41
Scotland, 143, 169
Scranton, 47
Second Mountain, 144
Selinsgrove, 9, 75, 119, 127, 135, 137
Seneca Indians, 19
Seven Mountains, 109
Shadbush (illustrated), 125
Shade Mountain, 110, 191
Shamokin, 17, 19, 22, 122, 135
Shamokin Creek, 127
Shamokin Dam, 118, 172
Shaver Creek, 105
Shawnee Indians, 97
Shawville, 60
Shenk's Ferry, 206
Sherman Creek, 145
Sheshequin Town, 29, 30
Shickshinny, 43, 45, 46, 51
Shickshinny Creek, 51
Shikellamy, Chief, 25, 59, 91, 109, 120, 122, 127, 141
Shikellamy Cliff, 117
Shikellamy profile, 118
Shikellamy Town, 22, 88
Shoemaker, Colonel Henry W., 83

Shoemaker, Dr. Henry S., 113
Sideling Hill, 100, 101
Singmaster, Paul, 9
Sinking Spring Valley, 101, 102
Sinnemahoning, 83
Sinnemahoning Creek, 57, 191
Sipes, William, 103
Six Nations, 18, 22, 59, 91, 151
Skeer's Ferry, 154
Skinner's Eddy, 37
Slocum, Frances, 27, 40
Smith, Captain John, 3, 17
Smith, Provost William, 107
Snyder County, 69, 137
Somerset County, 93
South Carolina, 122
Southey, Robert, 115
South Mountain, 187
Spanish Hill, 17
Springer, J. Herbert, 9
Spruce Creek, 105
Standing Stone, 24, 33
Standing Stone (at Huntingdon), 107
Star Rock, 198
Starrucca Creek, 11, 12, 191
State Museum, 201
Steelton, 170, 175, 177, 178, 180
Stevenson, Robert Louis, xi
Stevens, Thaddeus, 97, 217
St. Lawrence River, 81
Storrick, Nina, 9
Strait of Magellan, 71
Strong, Dr. W. W., 201
Sullivan County, 89
Sullivan, General, 20, 29, 34, 41, 59
Sullivan Highlands, 89
Sullivan Trail, 33, 34, 38
Summit, 81
Sunbury, 17, 50, 57, 71, 75, 89, 114, 116, 117, 118, 122, 123, 125, 127, 131, 135, 172, 182, 208, 217
Surveyor, 61
Susquehanna and Tidewater Canal, 194, 197, 216
Susquehanna Canal, 101, 113, 139, 165
Susquehanna County, 13, 47, 193
Susquehanna University, 127
Susquehannock Indians, 3, 195
Sutcliffe, Robert, 193
Sutton, Dr. George Miksch, 9
Swatara Creek, 17, 177, 182
Switzerland, 203

Tahashwangarorus Indians, 19
Talon, Omer, 33
Tanacharison, Chief, 151

235

Theiss, Dr. Lewis, 173
Tiadaghton Creek, 87
Tiadaghton Elm, 76
Tilsbury's Knob, 42
Tioga Creek, 13
Tioga Point, 6, 13, 14, 17, 18, 20, 27, 29, 30, 34, 137
Tocanuntie Indians, 19
Tonkin, Joseph Dudley, 66, 71
Towanda, 23, 33, 167
Towanda Creek, 30, 89
Trenton, N. J., 154
Trevorton, 133, 135
Trip Lake, 13
Tucquan Club, 216
Tucquan Creek, 3, 203
Tulpehocken, 177
Tunkhannock, 32, 35, 39
Tunkhannock Creek, 30, 39
Turkey Hill, 197, 198
Turkey Ridge, 111
Turkeyville Falls, 214
Tuscarora Creek, 110, 111
Tuscarora Indians, 19
Tuscarora Mountain, 110, 111, 113, 191
Tuscarora Valley, 110
Tussey Mountain, 101, 105
Tyannuntasacta (Endless Hills), 21
Tyrone, 101, 103

Union County, 55, 76

Vandersloot, John E., 207
Vermont, 217
Virginia, 18, 22, 25, 141
Viscose Company, The, 106
von Zinzendorf, Count, 25, 59

Wake Robin (illustrated), 204
Walhalla, 87
Wallace, Dr. Paul A. W., 19, 25
Walnut Island, 201
Wapwallopen, 46
Wapwallopen Creek, 51
Warrior Path, 14
Warriors Mark, 107
Warrior Trail, 96
Washington, 176, 209
Washington, General George, 29, 57, 95, 151, 153, 154
Waterford, N. Y., 154, 209
Water Street, 96, 101
Watsontown, 86

Wayne, Anthony, 97
Webster, Daniel, 97
Weiser, Conrad, 17, 18, 19, 21, 22, 25, 27, 59, 120, 121, 122, 127, 151, 177
Weld, Isaac, Jr., 30
West Fairview, xiv, 160
West Nanticoke, 42
West Pittston, 37
West Shore Aquatic Club, 159
West Virginia, 62
Whiskey Rebellion, 97
White Deer, 86
White Deer Creek, 91
White Pine (illustrated), 68
Wiconisco Creek, 127
Wild Cat Glen, 189
Wilkes-Barre, 9, 27, 29, 30, 31, 34, 38, 40, 41, 51, 171, 186
Wilkes, John, 51
Williamsport, 62, 65, 71, 73, 75, 77, 78, 79, 80, 81, 89, 131, 163, 166
Williamsport Library, 9
Williams Valley, 133
Willis, N. P., 8, 163
Will Mountain, 101
Wilson, Alexander, 11
Wisconsin, 87
Womelsdorf, 17, 19, 21, 122
Wrightsville, 154, 189, 192, 193, 194, 196, 201, 228
Wyalusing, 30, 227
Wyalusing Creek, 3, 13, 30
Wyalusing Path, 28
Wyalusing Rocks, 28, 34
Wyoming, 51
Wyoming County, 37, 39
Wyoming Valley, 27, 39, 40, 44, 47, 48, 55, 57, 195
Wysox, 33
Wysox Creek, 30

Yellow Breeches Creek, 191, 201
York, 59, 179, 181, 187
York County, 4, 183, 184, 188, 190, 192, 202, 216, 217, 228
York Haven, 171, 179, 181, 182, 184, 186, 187, 189, 224
York Haven Dam, 181
York Hills, 151
Yorktown, 33
York Y. M. C. A., 211, 212
Young Woman's Town, 87